Other Books by Victor C. Bolles

Principled Policy, A Conversation about America

Tawantinsuyu, A novel about nuclear terror

The Edifice of Trust

Second Edition

Toward a Principled Social Policy

By Victor C. Bolles

Copyright © by Victor C. Bolles

All rights reserved. No part of this book may be reproduced in any form or by any electronic or mechanical means, including information storage and retrieval systems, without permission in writing from the publisher except by a reviewer who may quote brief passages in a review.

Table of Contents

Chapter 1: A Foundation of Principles   1
Chapter 2: The Edifice of Trust   22
Chapter 3: Race Relations   36
Chapter 4: Changing Demographics   55
Chapter 5: Gender as a Political Tool   72
Chapter 6: Foreign Trade and Employment   93
Chapter 7: Education: The Path to Opportunity   104
Chapter 8: Is Healthcare a Civil Right?   118
Chapter 9: Gun Violence   130
Chapter 10: Terror   141
Chapter 11: What Works   146

Foreword

I wrote the first edition of this book to discuss the great issues upon which I thought the 2016 presidential elections would hinge. The economy had been under-performing ever since the Great Recession of 2008, the public debt was almost $20 trillion (that's with a T folks!), Russian troops were in the Ukraine, the Chinese were building artificial islands in the South China Sea and fortifying them with ships and planes, Turkey's democracy was being overthrown by its Prime Minister and the cancer of ISIS was metastasizing. So obviously, I thought the key issues on which the US election would turn would be domestic social issues.

That's what happened in the 2012 election. The economy was in even worse shape than in 2016, public debt was skyrocketing, Islamic militants had just assassinated the US Ambassador and three other diplomats in Libya, and the North Koreans had launched a satellite into space. So what were the key issues on which the 2012 election turned? It was whether female college students had to pay for their own contraceptive medications or whether you and I should pay for them through our current taxes (or our children and grandchildren will pay for them by servicing the public debt).

Not that Mrs. Clinton did not try and get the election to revolve around social issues. She had her army of progressive warriors ready to wage strident warfare on the social issue front - everything from bathroom transgender policy to defunding Planned Parenthood. But she barely had time to get around to these issues as she had to keep defending herself from the constant attacks from Candidate Trump and the leaks and hacks from her own organization.

But don't think for a minute that social issues will go gentle into that good night. They will rage, rage against the dying of the light (to steal a phrase from Dylan Thomas). We are seeing that rage across the country as progressives pack the town hall meetings of Republican congressmen to push their progressive social agenda. So there is still validity in analyzing social issues from a principled perspective.

We have social problems in the US. There is no doubt about it. Race relations appear to be at an all-time low even though Americans have elected a black president, twice. Black teenagers have to be given the "talk" (of how to not get shot by a policeman). Meanwhile, police officers are being ambushed across the country. The Federal government is trying to force schools that accept federal funds (just about all of them) to open the bathrooms to a person's gender identification no matter what it says down there below the waistline. The Supreme Court has put its blessing on same-sex marriage. Can polygamy be right around the corner?

There is a welter of opinions about these issues. Some of these opinions are labeled liberal and some are labeled conservative. But you can bet none of these opinions can be labeled principled. Until now. This book intends to take on these issues from the perspective of the founding principles of the United States. The Founders didn't address many of these issues directly. I don't think the concept of a transgender person ever entered the mind of George Washington. (Not that they didn't exist. There were a lot of spinsters and lifelong bachelors back then.)

As no one else seems to be willing to, I propose to develop a set of positions on these issues that are logically consistent, can be inferred from America's founding principles and can be subscribed to by the American people. It is difficult to apply logic and rational thought to many of these issues. You could see the emotional strain in the face and voice of Senator Tim Scott when he got up on the floor of the Senate and discussed the discrimination he faced and the shame and confusion he felt. These aren't political issues. They are emotional issues and, sometimes, medical issues, which is why they carry more weight in the polling booth than economics or international diplomacy.

Many people think that America has been going in the wrong direction. Right now about half the country is looking to President Trump to change that direction while the other half has vowed to oppose everything President Trump stands for and drive a left-wing social agenda.

But without a set of principles, how will we know which direction to go? That is why I have updated Edifice of Trust with this second edition.

Victor Bolles
March 1, 2017

Edifice of Trust

Chapter 1

A Foundation of Principles

Coming to Terms with Terminology

How we understand things is determined (at least in part) by words. We have to agree on the meaning of words – the definitions -- so that we can understand each other. The problem is that our words can have many definitions and they sometimes overlap or contradict one another, or mean different things to different people. In the political sphere we have a plethora of terms many of which confuse and divide us. The advent of the Trump presidency may require that we redefine what it means to be a Republican. Bernie Sanders tried to redefine what it means to be a Democrat and, to a large extent, was successful. So how are we supposed to come together if we don't share common definitions of terms? How else can we know what the other person is talking about? For this book, I will try and assign meanings to many terms that are flung about in political discussions. You may not agree with my definitions but at least you should be able to understand what I am talking about.

Edifice of Trust

I think our confusion got started with the term liberal. If you read Adam Smith and the Economist magazine, a liberal would be a person who believed in personal liberty, democracy and free markets. That would be very different from how a right wing person in the US today would define the term liberal. And what's this thing about right wing and left wing anyway?

Right-wing/Left-wing

The concept of left-wing and right-wing came from France (this is beginning to make sense to me now). In eighteenth century France, monarchists and conservatives who favored order sat on the right side of the Estates-General (legislative assembly) and the revolutionaries and reformists who favored change sat on the left. The terms left-wing and right-wing were not commonly used outside of France until the twentieth century. In the United States left-wing has come to mean people who prefer big government or communal solutions to social and economic problems and right-wing means people who prefer limited government, greater personal liberty and traditional social values.

Party politics and the terms used to define them have evolved over time to the extent that they often bear little resemblance to their original meanings. There are also gradations and overlap of these general terms. These general terms also have sub-categories -- more specific meanings that are affiliated with specific groups of people. Trotskyites, for example, were a faction of the Communist Party. Trotsky differed from party orthodoxy but was still a Communist. Stalin killed him and sent his followers to the Gulag (definition of gulag: forced-labor camps in Siberia).

Commentary

Government, by its nature, uses coercive power over its citizens to benefit the greater society. As a result our freedoms are constrained when we live in a society with other men and women. The question that we must answer is how much coercive state power provides the maximum benefit to society and to the individuals within that society. Leftists believe that more state power

Edifice of Trust

(bigger government) will achieve this goal while right-wingers believe that less government is more beneficial. These goals can also be viewed on at least two different levels; the material (wealth transfer vs. wealth creation) and the psychological (security vs. empowerment).

On the Left

The left favors big government and government solutions to social problems and has identified many social ills such as gender issues, civil rights and income inequality as left wing or progressive issues. Left of center can range from those favoring unions and progressive taxation to the social welfare state that requires a large amount of income redistribution all the way to the government owning the means of production.

Democrats

The current Democratic Party traces its origins back to the Republican-Democratic faction led by Thomas Jefferson and other (mostly southern) Founders. But this Jeffersonian faction bears little resemblance to the current Democratic Party. Recall that it was anti-government, agrarian and believed in states' rights and slavery. It was Democratic Governor Orville Faubus that resisted Republican President Dwight Eisenhower's attempt to integrate Little Rock Central High School. Democrats edged more to the left under Kennedy and then more so under Johnson's War on Poverty (which has made very little progress in the fifty years since). The Democrats have slowly become more left wing over time until an avowed socialist ran and almost won the primary battle to be the Democratic candidate for president.

Progressives

The Progressive movement began in the late-Nineteenth century with an agenda of trust busting, breaking up monopolies and rooting out corruption in government (these interrelated issues feed on each other). But these proscribed activities all violate the social contract and as such are not left or right issues but issues of good governance. Over time progressives took on other causes that appeared neutral (such as conservation, ending child labor and public education) but that led them leftward. Now the progressive wing of the Democratic Party is considered further left than the mainstream.

Socialists

Socialists believe that government should own the means of production for many industries so that they can function for the public good and not for making a profit. It is an outgrowth of Marxist thought but asserts that a mixed economy can best serve the people; giving government control of industries serving the public good but allowing citizens the ability run businesses that are not essential. The problem is that this relationship is not static and government tends to crowd out and the take over the private sector. The public and private sectors do not operate by the same rules, which gives a competitive advantage to the rule maker (i.e.; government).

Nordic Social Democracy

While socialism has a miserable economic and political track record, the social democratic regimes of the Nordic countries have posted an enviable record. Government plays a large role in these countries (near or over 50% of GDP) while still having a fairly robust private sector. Taxes are high but the people are generally happy with their social welfare schemes. In analyzing Nordic Social Democracy you may want to emphasize Nordic over Social. These countries are relatively homogenous and share a common culture and traditional religion. Even so, the stresses being felt in the rest of Europe are beginning to be felt in the north as some countries cut back social programs for budgetary reasons. Large numbers of Middle Eastern refugees have caused some countries to cut back on the generous benefits previously offered to immigrants and refugees.

Edifice of Trust

Marxist/Communist
Karl Marx was outraged at the working conditions of laborers in the early industrial revolution. He felt that wealthy capitalists exploited the labor of their workers in order to make a profit (providing them with more capital to exploit more workers). To remedy this problem he proposed that the government control all the means of production. But if government is to control the means of productions and production is to be determined by a central planning committee, the government cannot be subject to the whims of a gullible electorate thus requiring an absolute dictatorship.

On the Right
The right favors limited government and lower taxes. However, supply side economics based on the Laffer Curve theory has not generated sufficient growth to offset the lower tax rates resulting in increased fiscal deficits. This is called trickle down economics by the left who state that the wealth increases accrue to the "one percent", who leave very little to trickle down to the rest of the population.

Republicans
The Republican Party was formed in 1854 by abolitionists and ex-Whigs to try to defeat the Democratic Party that had dominated the United States government in the antebellum period and was especially strong in the South. The Republicans were opposed to slavery and the election of Republican Abraham Lincoln precipitated the Civil War. Today the Republican Party is identified (mostly by Democrats) as controlled by corporate interests and Wall Street (who actually try to control both parties). The Republicans mostly favor lower taxes, limited government and conservative values (social and fiscal).

Conservatives
Conservatives believe in Anglo/American traditional values infused with the Judeo-Christian belief system. Many believe in religious based values and strongly oppose abortion and same-sex marriage for that reason. Because many

of their beliefs are scripturally based, they are less amenable to secular arguments and less likely to change opinions on issues. They are confronted by a gradual secularization of the American people (due to demographic and cultural changes) that has resulted in erosion of the acceptance of many of their values. Most conservatives will be found in the Republican Party but there are Conservative Parties in some states for mostly local races.

Fiscal and Social Conservatives

Many politicians claim to be fiscal conservatives although in reality they rarely are. Even the Republicans under the Bush administration pushed through Medicare Part D, a budget busting benefit for senior citizens. Whether it is Democratic spending and Republican tax cutting, few politicians are actually fiscally conservative. On social issues there is a clearer divide. In order to actually be fiscally conservative our politicians in Washington, DC will require a Balanced Budget Amendment to restrain future deficits.

Libertarians

There is a Libertarian Party, which regularly runs candidates for local, state and national elections although they rarely win. Libertarians often vote Republican and closely resemble the members of the Tea Party at least on fiscal issues. Libertarians are fiscal conservatives and believe in a very limited government but are not strong social conservatives. They believe people have the right to do anything that does not infringe on the rights of others. They generally shun a strong foreign policy (and foreign aid) and reject participation in foreign wars unless American interests are directly affected.

The Tea Party

There are actually many Tea Parties scattered across the country. The Tea party is an amalgam of grass roots movements that arose following the bank bailouts by the administration of President Obama in response to the financial crisis of 2008. The local Tea Party organizations have differing and often conflicting agendas ranging between libertarian, populist and conservative. Although they are a relatively small part of the electorate they can have a disproportionate impact in primary elections dragging the Republican Party further to the right, just as the progressives are dragging the Democratic Party to the left.

Other Terms
Some political movements are hard to place on the left-right continuum.

Liberals
I try to refrain from using the term "liberal" because it is too confusing unless I apply an adjective such as "classical liberal" to further define the term. In the US, liberals are considered to be toward the left and are associated with tax and spend policies. US liberals are the counter to US conservatives (spendthrifts vs. tightwads). Classic liberals (such as the magazine The Economist) are for free markets and free trade. America was founded based on classical liberal philosophy that emphasized free markets, free trade, the rule of law and representative democracy. Many of these concepts are embedded in the Constitution and our other democratic institutions.

Populist/Populism
Populism can also be called majoritarianism in that it appeals to a majority within a country by addressing their interests while ignoring or repressing the interests of minorities (keeping in mind that there are many ways to slice and dice a population to define majorities and minorities). Populism appeals to the majority by alienating minorities in order to garner votes. And it blames the minorities for any problems. It often attacks elites especially if they are from an ethnic minority such as Jews in Nazi Germany or ethnic Chinese in Malaysia. It provides benefits to the majority through the use of state power. Populism can be either left wing or right wing but it tends toward authoritarianism because of the need to wield state power. In a leftist populist state the government would take over the means of production. In a right wing

populist state the government would control the means of production through fear and repression (also the confiscation of minority property).

Nationalist/Nationalism

Nationalism appeals to the pride citizens feel about their country. The government hopes that by closely associating the country with the government that the citizens will also look favorably on the government. By focusing on nationalism, the government hopes that citizens will ignore its failures to deliver in other areas such as economic growth. Nationalism is also not a left or right issue. The two most nationalistic countries now are Russia and China where leaders are fomenting friction with enemies (the US and its allies) to justify their actions at home. The failing state of Venezuela blames enemies and saboteurs for the current economic crisis calling it an economic war.

Fascist/Fascism (Nazi/Nazism)

Fascism is mostly identified as right wing because of its authoritarianism and nationalism. But this does not have much relevance to US right-wing politics. Fascist authoritarianism requires a large and powerful state with substantial control of the means of production especially in military hardware and industries critical to national defense (many forget that Nazi stands for National Socialist German Workers party and that Mussolini was a socialist before he was a fascist). Fascist states often operate on a war footing, which justifies their authoritarianism and is closely related to nationalism and populism.

Keynesians

John Maynard Keynes was a British economist who developed a general theory of employment, interest and money. One part of this theory asserts that government can influence the economy by spending money, even money that it does not have (deficit spending). He felt that counter-cyclical spending by government could mitigate the impact of a downturn in the economy by giving money to workers to generate economic activity. Further, there was a multiplier effect since the money that workers spent (for example, to buy food) would subsequently be spent by other workers to generate even more economic activity (for example, the farmer who grew the food), and so on. Although Keynes also believed in counter-cyclical savings (surpluses) during periods of economic growth, politicians have never seen a period of sufficient economic growth and so spend continuously resulting in a public debt of approximately $20 trillion (a process that caused Republican President Richard Nixon to say "we are all Keynesians now").

Freidrich Hayek and the Chicago Boys

Freidrich Hayek was an economist of the Austrian School. He felt that government involvement in the economy distorted prices and resulted in sub-optimal economic growth. He argued that government involvement in the economy inevitably led to authoritarianism and tyranny. His academic career ultimately led him to the University of Chicago where he, along with Milton Friedman and others trained a generation of Latin American economists labeled the Chicago Boys. The Chicago Boys are credited with instituting economic reforms during the Pinochet regime that transformed Chili into the fastest growing economy in the region.

Behavioral Economics

Behavioral economics has put a wrench into mainstream economic theory. Most economic theory requires that people act rationally (although even Keynes admitted that they don't always do so). The progenitors of behavioral economics (Daniel Kahneman and Amos Tversky, both psychologists) showed through a series of experiments that people have built-in biases and instincts that affect their economic thinking, such as loss aversion (losing a dollar hurts more than gaining a dollar pleases). These inborn biases also affect our political decisions (taller candidates such as Mr. Trump have a decided advantage over shorter rivals).

Edifice of Trust

Principle-based Politics

The above list is a compendium of the political and economic groups and thought trends taken into account in writing this book. You may not agree with the definitions that I have included above but that is not the point. Whether you agree with my definitions or not, knowing my definitions will help you understand what I am trying to say and that understanding is the basis for dialogue.

It is hard to categorize the principles I have used in my books according to the terms listed above. I start by outlining principles on which to base the social contract and then follow them through to their logical conclusions. Of, course, if you have different principles you will end up with different logical conclusions. The principles on which this book is based are the Enlightenment principles expressed by Thomas Jefferson in the Declaration of Independence: life, liberty and the pursuit of happiness (although when John Locke first wrote down these principles it was life, liberty and property).

Why should our economic and political lives be guided by principles? Throughout history societies have been governed by cultural and religious traditions. These traditions often expressed universal principles that would be applicable to any people but others were unique to a particular people and not translatable to other cultures. America was formed by Christian Europeans and our culture and its institutions reflect that heritage. But America is home to people of different origins and different religions and cultures. I believe that Enlightenment principles, although grafted from this Christian, European heritage, are universal and can be accepted by people of many different traditions, religions and cultures (although perhaps not all).

Western Civilization and its Values

Western Civilization is the product of European political and cultural development over the last two and a half thousand years. Like all other great civilizations it has striven to reach the heights of culture and the arts and wallowed in the deepest pits of human depravity. Although born in paganism, Western Civilization soon joined Greek principles of democracy and rationalism

Edifice of Trust

with Christian concepts of the value of individuals as made in God's image to form a cultural and religious heritage that survives to this day. The Christian religion also went through dark its times. But both the civilization and the religion have emerged from its dark periods to articulate a more enlightened view of the world and the people in it.

Western culture has reached its present state under the leadership of the United States during the period since the end of World Wars One and Two. The Anglosphere (English speaking) countries developed these democratic principles and other Enlightenment values that are now ascendant around the world. But there are other cultures and beliefs among the so-called Western nations that make up most of the advanced economies around the world (Japan has a very different culture, religion and history but has adopted many of these principles). All of these different but similar cultures make up what we call the West or Western Civilization.

The United States has incorporated these Enlightenment values into its culture even more than the other English speaking countries so that certain aspects are uniquely American although they may exist in other Western countries to a certain degree or in another form. In this book, when I refer to Western civilization I am referring to the broader Western culture shared by many nations around the globe, and when I speak of American principles or values I am speaking of the uniquely American interpretation of Western culture as practiced in the US.

And although we Americans have not always faithfully adhered to these principles (like some have not faithfully adhered to their religion) it is to these principles that we aspire. Although we are not perfect we believe in perfectibility: our ability to make things better.

When addressing social problems many people want to do "good" and be "fair". But without a base of sound principles these do-good efforts can drift. President Obama employed a "what works" philosophy where he would not discriminate between socialist and capitalist systems as long as the solution "works" (this was after his trip to Cuba). The Democratic candidates in the 2016 election also promoted "what works" solutions to social problems cloaking them

Edifice of Trust

as true to American values. But socialist solutions to problems are not based on American values and principles; they are based on Marxist principles. We can always debate principles but disguising Marxist principles as American is just a magician's parlor trick. This book does not subscribe to such moral equivalency and asserts that the American Founding Principles are the best fit for our country.

So now that we have established a set of defined terms that we can discuss reasonably and rationally let us move on to defining the principles that will be the basis for our society and form the key elements of the American Social Contract.

Edifice of Trust

American Principles Restated

If we want a principled government, then we need to have a clear idea of what those principles are. Here are my ideas of the principles on which the American Social contract is based.

The Right to Life

The Declaration of Independence asserts our right to "life, liberty and the pursuit of happiness" (Jefferson converted Locke's right to property to the pursuit of happiness – we will deal with property later). If we do not have a right to life, we have no rights at all.

It is passing strange that the left wants to give the right to life to convicted murderers by eliminating the death penalty but to take it from innocent fetuses. But they have a point. Given the number of people on death row that have been later found innocent, I would assert that the death penalty should be abolished. Benjamin Franklin commented (based on Blackstone's well-known formulation) that "it is better 100 guilty Persons should escape than that one innocent Person should suffer". But shouldn't innocent fetuses be granted the same privilege? If we are going to live our lives based on principles, shouldn't they be applied consistently?

Personal Liberty/Personal Responsibility

Our personal liberty is based on our natural rights as envisioned by Locke and other Enlightenment philosophers. In order to create the social

Edifice of Trust

contract that facilitates our ability to live with other human beings, we cede certain rights and powers to government and assign government the responsibility of maintaining the social contract. Benjamin Franklin warned about ceding any of our "essential" liberties to government and the need to assure that government only had limited powers. Personal liberty is very individualistic and American individualism has been one of our most noted national characteristics.

Progressives want to demote individualism and to raise up communalism. They state that the community or society is more important than the individual and that individual rights must be subjugated to the needs of the community. This is a very Hobbesian form of the social contract. You purchase your safety and security within the social contract with your liberty. This is the bargain that progressives are offering to the American people.

With personal liberty comes personal responsibility. If you are free you are responsible for taking care of your needs, earning a living, providing housing and food for you and your family. You are responsible for taking care of your health and saving for the future. In the classic (1974) book, *The Unheavenly City Revisited*, Edward Banfield showed that the principle difference between wealthy people and poor people was the ability to plan for the future. The poor have very short-term time horizons thereby condemning themselves to continued poverty. Progressives want to relieve you of this responsibility by having the government take responsibility for your healthcare, your retirement, your day-to-day needs. But in doing that, the government also takes your liberty. It would be more difficult to educate the poor on extending their time horizons. Just give them (other peoples') money and the problem goes away. Doesn't it?

Free Market Economics

Personal liberty also requires economic liberty. The free market existed long before Adam Smith first described it in The Wealth of Nations. No matter how hard various monarchs and dictators have tried to suppress free markets, they keep popping up wherever the enforcers' gaze is turned the other way. It

Edifice of Trust

might be called a black market by the oppressive authorities but it is a spontaneous and natural human reaction to economic incentives.

But a free market doesn't give a person the right to lie or cheat in economic transactions. Whenever a person lies about the nature of a product or cheats someone, they are denying the other person the right to receive what they are paying for. The economic role of government in the social contract is to assure citizens that they can trust the honesty of the counterparts in economic transactions and other human interactions. And if the counterparty proves untrustworthy, the government has courts empowered to issue judgments or remedies for the injured party.

Progressives want economic transactions to serve the needs of the community however they might determine those needs to be. Your right to buy a red car or blue car (color selection is so bourgeois. Use public transportation.) is subordinated to the needs of the greater community

Private Property

Locke felt that private property was essential to freedom. If a person is not secure in what he or she creates, how can that person be said to have any rights at all? If a person creates something such as a work of art, how can that person be said to have any rights if that creation can be taken from them by government or another person? Likewise if you create value by working for someone and receive money and then use that money to purchase something, you need to be secure in your ownership of whatever you purchased. Without that security why would anyone invest the time or money in creating anything?

Citizens of a social contract cede to the government the ability to tax, which is a taking of private property. This cession is supposedly voluntary. Without the ability to tax, the government cannot function. So this cession is an essential part of the social contract. Citizens, however, retain the right to change governments and can do so if the taxes are deemed too onerous.

Progressives distort this cession of the government's ability to tax citizens. President Obama famously said "you didn't build that" saying that without government infrastructure and other benefits it would be impossible

Edifice of Trust

for an individual to create anything. He later walked back that comment by stating that people still had property rights. But progressives don't really believe that. They believe communal rights supersede individual rights. Seizing property is one of the first things that socialist regimes do when they come to power (the other is to eliminate independent trade unions).

Equal Opportunity

Personal liberty and equality of opportunity are inseparable. A person cannot be considered free if that person doesn't have the same opportunity as other people. If a person is not allowed to buy a home or get a job because of any type of discrimination, that person is not free. But equality of opportunity goes against human nature. Everyone is trying to get an "edge" or an "upper hand" or some other advantage in order to improve his or her chances of success. Parents send their kids to the best private schools. The athletic or good-looking try to take advantage of these gifts in sports or entertainment. The wealthy try to give their offspring a big inheritance or a family business. Those are not only normal impulses but also things that must be allowed in a free society. So total equality of opportunity is impossible to achieve (just like we cannot have perfect freedom but must allow other people a level of freedom as well). But it is our duty as a society to try and give everyone as much opportunity as possible. We can do this by ending discrimination and providing excellent education for all citizens. These are not easy things to do but we must always strive for these goals.

The progressives will tell you that the proof of opportunity is in the numbers. That it is "unfair" if one group is under represented in a profession or a neighborhood: that this underrepresentation is proof of discrimination. But people are different and have different interests. Numbers don't tell the whole story. Nobody would go to a NBA game if blacks were proportionately represented (1.8 players per team). John H. Miller in his book, *A Crude Look at the Whole*, uses the Schelling segregation model with 360 agents to show that randomly dispersed agents with only a slight algorithmic preference will tend to become highly segregated. This is why people live in certain neighborhoods, choose certain professions or like certain music. They are self-segregating. Going strictly by the numbers would, in the words of progressives, be "unfair".

Rule of Law/Equality before the Law

In America we live by the rule of law and not of man. But there are some conditions to this rule of law. The laws must be reasonable and considered by the people to be so (I.e.; not too "unfair"). Unreasonable laws will be rejected by the people and ignored. Only the coercive power of the state can enforce unreasonable laws. Dictatorships have many laws but require black shirts and secret police to enforce them. Democratic governments must rely on the acceptance of laws through a consensus of the people so that excessive force is not required for most people to abide by the law. Because laws are enacted by the elected representatives of the people, there is a presumption of the peoples' approval. If the representatives of the people pass unpopular or unreasonable laws they will be voted out of office. The complexity of today's laws makes it difficult for the people to understand the laws being enacted on their behalf so there has been an erosion in the trust in government and of the rule of law.

Laws also need to be enforced. Impunity breeds contempt for the rule of law. In Latin America (I don't mean to pick on Latin America but I lived there a long time and so have picked up many examples) people routinely run red lights. But police rarely stop a driver for running a red light so people ignore the law. In America, people will wait at a red light even if there is no one else around for miles. An exception is turning right on red right, which people routinely did. Most states changed the law to allow right turns on red because to not do so would be considered unreasonable.

Everybody needs to be equal before the law. This can be a hard objective to achieve. Rich people can afford to hire high-priced attorneys when in court but poor people can't. In the US, poor people accused of committing a crime can have a lawyer appointed for them and paid for by the government. That is a good attempt to level the playing field but it comes up short as the court-appointed lawyers are rarely as good as the high-priced one. In civil cases, rich people and corporations have a distinct advantage. There are some reforms that we could enact to increase the equality before the law (for example: requiring the losing side of a civil dispute to pay for the legal fees of the winner as is done in England so that wealthy people and corporations can't so easily intimidate opponents). But we can never achieve true equality before the law. Like many of our ideal principles we must make compromises when our principles conflict or our human nature intrudes. But compromise is the essence of the social contract, not perfection.

The "what works" philosophy of progressives subordinates the rule of law to the needs of the state, as Pfizer found out to its chagrin. President Obama used executive orders to circumvent a law (as in the Pfizer case) as well as to create law without legislative approval (as he attempted to do for the Dreamers). During the campaign, both Mr. Trump and Mrs. Clinton said they would use executive orders to implement their campaign promises if they had to. President Obama contemptuously told Republicans "I won. Get use to it", to which the Republicans should have responded "But we won the legislature, get used to that." But they didn't.

Minority Rights/Compassion for the Less Fortunate

Minority rights are important not because we like minorities but because we like freedom. The only way we can assure our own freedom is by making sure that a majority cannot take the rights of any individual or minority. It was a majority that kept blacks subjected to Jim Crow laws that discriminated against them. It was a majority of people in Europe that discriminated against Jews for centuries. The Founders sought to avoid this dictatorship of the majority by putting numerous checks and balances in the Constitution, and to elevate the Constitution, including the Bill of Rights, as the supreme law of the land.

Even with minority rights and equality of opportunity, there are some people that will not be able to fully participate in a free society. They may have ill health or a physical disability, mental health problems or some other factor that inhibits their ability to participate. These people deserve our compassion

Edifice of Trust

and assistance. The just society that we are trying to create could have it no other way. And there is a role that government can play in helping these people. But there are other groups that also can be of assistance such as churches and charitable organizations. Government should only intervene in cases where there are gaps in care provided by these civic organizations. The government should not crowd out these institutions with excessive requirements as it has been doing. This lessens the civic participation of the people and divides them from their fellow citizens[1].

The position of the progressives is that all people need government assistance. That every one needs welfare checks, pensions, healthcare, child rearing assistance or other government mandated programs that take money from one group and give it to another.

It is easy to create a Hobbesian state. All the people need is the ability to endure the boot heel of oppressive government. The secret police will take care of the few who resist. It is much more difficult to create a Lockean democratic government. Our inability to create a society as we envision is indicative of our human frailty rather than a denunciation of our lofty dreams.

But what about Conservatives?

It is true that I haven't compared conservative positions with our American principles as I have to the progressives. One reason is that conservatism, by its nature, is closer ideologically to our founding principles. The problem with conservatives is that they look at issues based on tradition or religion in order to formulate their policies. As a result their arguments may be unconvincing to people who do not share the same traditions or religion. America is becoming more diverse and less religious so conservative efforts to govern have become less effective. Instead conservatives need to look deeper into the philosophical reasons behind the political principles they espouse in order to convince a more diverse population of the rightness of their cause.

---

1. For a good discussion of the erosion of US civil society, please read <u>The Great Degeneration</u>, by Niall Ferguson.

Edifice of Trust

Also, conservatives misunderstand what drives economic growth and the role of regulation. Economic growth is the Holy Grail for eliminating deficits and beginning to pay down our enormous public debt. Tax cuts don't drive economic growth. Cutting taxes is just as ineffective in the long run as excessive government spending in creating the growth needed to eliminate deficits and to reduce the debt. A lack of principled regulation increases the volatility of the economy just as excessive regulation stifles it. The role of principled regulation of the economy is to build trust that facilitates economic growth by creating a consistent and reasonable set of rules acceptable to the people. If the progressives want to do "what works", conservatives want to do "what used to work". They just don't understand why fighting the last war is not a good way to build the future.

And then there is President Trump

President Trump began his presidency by issuing a slew of executive orders honoring his campaign promises made during a heated, dirty campaign. Keeping promises is a principled thing to do but the promises were not made on principles. They were often made by appealing to the lowest common denominator and not the highest principle. Many were made off the cuff on the spur of the moment during famously unscripted campaign rallies.

Although it is early in his term as president, he appears to be more interested in winning than in doing the right thing. He is a businessman and he looks at issues on a transactional basis. He wants to win on any issue or negotiation. But many of our international agreements are multivariate and any action will have implications far beyond the specific issue being discussed or negotiated. For example, on the issue of accepting refugees being held by Australia he had a very strained conversation with the Australian prime minister and threatened to renege on his predecessor's commitment to take the refugees. But Australia is one of our staunchest allies and it is unwise to undermine that relationship in order to win what is in essence a very minor point

Edifice of Trust

Because President Trump is transactional he looks at issues opportunistically. How to win a point or gain the upper hand on his opponent. But Australia and our other allies are not our opponents they are our friends and allies. Yes, it is true that most other NATO members do not live up to their financial or military obligations to this defense organization and that America undertakes the lion's share of the burden on keeping NATO a vital organization. But threatening to back out of NATO in order to motivate our allies to pay up is short sighted.

If President Trump is not going to base his actions and policy proposals on American principles then it will be up to his cabinet and the Congress to bear this burden. Trump's honeymoon period as president looked more like a WWF or MMA event than a honeymoon. And the American people want someone to shake up Washington and to make meaningful changes. President Trump is decisive but impulsive. He is in the process of tearing down the structure of democratic institutions but he has left us in the dark as to what the new structure will look like. Builders, of which President Trump must be counted, often have to tear down existing structures and clear land in order to construct a new building or complex. But, because no builder can erect a complex structure on his own, the builder must have a vision or plan that others can follow under his leadership to complete the project.

By adhering to the American principles outlined above, President Trump will be able to elaborate a vision to create a new structure of American politics that will serve the American people for generations to come.

The Edifice of Trust

How Trust Works

There are many men of principle in both parties in America, but there is no party of principle.
    -Alexis de Tocqueville

The edifice of the American Social Contract and its Free Market Economic System is built with bricks of trust. When we interact with fellow citizens we trust that we will be treated with respect and dignity. When we purchase a product or service we trust that the product is safe and healthy and that the service is as advertised.

However, because we are all human not all of our fellow citizens can live up to the level of trust that we extend to others and rightfully expect in return. Some people may not be capable of interacting at this level because of some physical or mental disability. Some may violate our trust due to unusual and temporary circumstances much like *Le Miserables'* Jean Valjean's initial crime of stealing bread for his starving family. Then there are people that don't trust others or believe in the social contract between citizens. These people will

Edifice of Trust

violate our trust for personal gain and try to distort the social contract to their advantage. The elite of the world seem to believe that the rules do not apply to them and suspicious people justify their actions by the supposed transgressions of others (because they assume others to have the same evil intentions that they have).

Sometimes we ourselves fail to live up to our own standards in our dealings with others. Then we try to rationalize our failings by pointing to our upbringing, education, experiences or other factors. But we are only human and these lapses occur from time to time. We can only hope to man up to our shortcomings, be forgiven and have an opportunity to re-earn the trust of our fellow citizens.

In a small, tight community we know all of our fellow citizens and their strengths and weaknesses. In a small community we know who to trust, who to forgive and who to wary of. In a small community, unworthy behavior is met with distrust and the unworthy individual will have a hard time living and working with his fellow citizens. In a huge country like the United States it is impossible to know everyone. It is impossible to forge the bonds of trust with so many millions. It is the job of government to build this edifice of trust.

Tribal Trust

Generally, we trust what we know and distrust what we don't know. In a small community it is possible to know all the individuals and to know which ones to trust. People from other communities or tribes are inherently distrusted until a bond of trust is established between the two groups. These bonds of trust are developed slowly by first extending trust in certain limited situations and then deciding if that extension of trust was justified.

Extending trust is a risky action. You don't know if the other person is trustworthy. It is easy to be deceived. So trust develops slowly over time and can be easily lost by a single disappointment. Small tribal communities are homogenous. The people speak the same language, they look and dress similarly (they are likely to be related), and they generally perceive the world in a similar way (they have a common culture and/or religion).

Edifice of Trust

In a tribal culture, the bond of trust only extends to other members of the tribe. Interactions with other tribes are done very carefully and conflict is very common. This is one reason why the Mideast has had such a difficult time in building democratic nation states. Tribal culture is very strong in the Middle East and the national borders established by France and England after the First World War often crisscrossed tribal lands without regard to the people living there. There are no bonds of trust between these squabbling tribes so the Middle Eastern nations require a strong man with an iron fist to keep the fractious tribes from going after each other. Egypt quickly retreated from its experiment with democracy and Turkey appears to be going the same direction.

Inclusive Trust

Extending trust to other communities thus encounters barriers such as language, dress or culture that must be overcome in order for trust to develop. In the Middle East these barriers have not been overcome. If one tribe or culture is dominant all the other tribes must be subordinate. They are outside the circle of trust that the dominant tribal members share and are literally second-class citizens.

A democratic nation cannot function this way. The bonds of trust must be extended to all trustworthy citizens despite barriers of culture or language. The conundrum of the United States is that it has done this both poorly and well at basically the same time. The US has been able to absorb millions upon millions of immigrants from many different countries and cultures and to gradually incorporate them into the circle of trust. Despite early discrimination and hardships Polish, Irish, Italian and Jewish immigrants have been brought into the circle of trust. For blacks and, to a somewhat lesser extent, Hispanics it has been another story.

Protests (some devolving into riots) during the summer of 2016 showed us the consequences of non-inclusive trust. People excluded from the circle of trust for whatever reason build their own circle of trust within their own community. This is one reason why gangs flourish and police are feared in many

Edifice of Trust

black communities. They function as an alternative circle of trust for alienated black youth.

To extend the circle of trust to include blacks and Hispanics and Muslims and homosexuals and Lesbians and whoever else is out there will be risky and likely fraught with conflict. The de-escalation training and community involvement of the Dallas Police Department could not stop a lone gunman from assassinating five of its officers. After hundreds of years of exclusion there will be resistance from the black community (and other alienated communities) to building the necessary levels of trust to reach out to the larger society.

This is not a left or right issue. This is not a Democrat or Republican issue. This is an American issue. The United States cannot become a welter of warring tribes of homogenous ethnicities or religions. We have principles that stand for something greater. We must embrace these principles, the American principles envisioned by our Founders, as a bridge to incorporate all those that believe in those principles.

Edifice of Trust

Trust in the Social Contract

The entire concept of the social contract is based on trust. In a Hobbesian natural world there is no trust. Its every man for himself, kill or be killed. Life in such a natural environment would be, according to Hobbes, "nasty, brutish and short". In Hobbes' mind this fearful alternative justified obedience to an all-powerful sovereign (a Leviathan) who would have the power to impose order.

Hobbes' natural world probably never really existed. People are social animals and like other primates our primitive ancestors probably gathered into small bands and familial groups for comfort and protection. But trust did not extend very far beyond this small group. Life back then was brutal. Archeologists have confirmed that the bones of our prehistoric ancestors often showed evidence of violence and even early forms of warfare.

Coming about forty years after Hobbes, John Locke had a different view of human society. He felt that humans living in a state of nature had natural rights. That when humans came together in groups they had to give up some of their natural rights when they conflicted with the rights of others. It takes a certain level of trust to give up natural rights. It is the trust that others in the group will not assert their natural rights after you have given up some of yours. The Lockean natural world was, like Hobbes', also a thought experiment rather than reality.

So we are left with two versions of the social contract. In the Hobbesian version, an all-powerful sovereign imposes the social contract on his or her

Edifice of Trust

subjects in order to overcome the distrust among the subjects. In the Lockean version, people voluntarily choose to associate with each other by including the other people within the edifice of trust among citizens. This, in essence, was the principal debate in the 2016 election: which vision of the social contract to pursue. Unfortunately, the two major party candidates both chose the Hobbesian version of our social contract. In one party the all-powerful sovereign was a classic populist strong man while in the other party the all-powerful sovereign was the federal government.

This Hobson's choice was inflicted upon us because of the apparently intransigent social problems that the country faces. We are beset by racial tensions, uncontrolled immigration, rising crime, gender issues, demographic changes, generational divides and unaffordable healthcare for our aging population. But these problems exist because of a lack of trust. Many in America feel that the social contract does not operate for everyone but rather for a special few. Trust is the mortar that holds together the edifice of our nation and our mortar is crumbling.

The Hobbesian version of the social contract does not rely on trust. It relies on power. Power to overwhelm distrust without dissipating it. But it is a facile choice. Distrust is crushed, not resolved. Without resolving the distrust overweening power must be applied continually for order to be maintained. This was how Saddam Hussein maintained power over the fractious factions and sects in Iraq. And this is why Iraq has seen unceasing violence since his overthrow. Our policy makers in Washington naively thought democracy, in and of itself, would resolve centuries of distrust. We are still paying for this miscalculation.

Actually resolving differences and building trust is much harder. It requires dialogue not force, although some force may be required temporarily if the alternative is violent confrontation. That is why president Eisenhower called out federal troops to counter efforts to block the integration of black students into Little Rock Central High School in 1957 following the Supreme Court's unanimous decision on Brown vs. the Board of Education.

Edifice of Trust

In 2016, I hear a lot of angry voices but very little dialogue. There are people in our country who are in a lot of pain from injustice and discrimination. It is the pain that Senator Tim Scott expressed on the Senate floor in his speeches on race relations. But after catharsis we must rebuild the edifice of trust among us. That will take reasoned dialogue and honesty rather than acrimony and insults. In this conversation we do not have all evil on one side and only good on the other. All stakeholders have their valid points that must be addressed. Will the end result be something that will make everyone perfectly happy? That is unlikely but that is not the purpose of the social contract. The purpose of the social contract is that we can live together, not that we agree on everything.

Edifice of Trust

The Role of Government

So what is the appropriate role of government in fostering the trust necessary for the operation of the social contract? Much of this depends on whether you take a Hobbesian or Lockean view of the social contract. Under the Hobbesian vision, the sovereign is a monarch or dictator whose government uses force to overcome the distrust among citizens. This is precisely the vision that was rejected by the Founders. (It is also the reason they included the Second Amendment, which Amendment is under attack by the forces that support the Hobbesian view.)

The colonists viewed King George III as a tyrant. The Declaration of Independence features a long list of all the abuses the colonists endured under his rule. Thomas Paine's pamphlet, *Common Sense* (1776), was a denunciation of the Leviathan of English monarchy.

Under the Lockean vision of the social contract, authority is derived from the people living within the contract and it is the people who determine the role and power of the government.

"*We the People of the United States*, in Order to form a more perfect Union, establish Justice, insure domestic Tranquility, provide for the common defense, promote the general Welfare, and secure the Blessings of Liberty to ourselves and our Posterity, *do ordain and establish this Constitution for the United States of America*. (Emphasis added)"

Edifice of Trust

The powers granted to the government by the people are intended to foster and encourage the development of the social contract, not be the social contract. As the country develops, the interactions between citizens (the social contract) will change over time. The role of government was not intended to be so flexible, which is why it is not easy to amend the Constitution.

Trust is an essential element in human interaction. Human interaction involves risk whether risk of personal safety, risk of economic loss or other risks that we face day-to-day. Trust mitigates that risk. If we trust in law enforcement we do not fear walking on the city streets and interacting with the people we meet. Without that trust we fear unknown consequences and therefore shun walking on city streets and avoid potentially harmful human interactions (but also the possibility of positive human interactions). You can see that fear (lack of trust) prevents us from building strong communities by limiting the number of positive human interactions that can occur. It is the police powers of government that are supposed to help build the level of trust and foster more beneficial human interactions.

If we trust the quality of the food in our local grocery store then we do not hesitate to purchase what we need. We trust the sanitary conditions of its preparation; we trust the description of ingredients; and we trust the number of calories of the products (as long as we carefully check the portion size). It is the government's inspection of the production processes of the food we eat, along with laws that require disclosure of ingredients and calories, that allow us to trust that we are purchasing healthful products (or if we purchase unhealthful products at least we know the extent of their unhealthfulness).

Likewise, we trust that the bank where we deposit our money is in sound financial condition due to financial regulations and regular inspections by regulatory authorities. If, despite these precautions, there is a problem at the bank we trust that our deposits are safe because they are guaranteed by the Federal Deposit Insurance Corporation (which is not funded by the taxpayers but by fees paid by the banks).

Absent trust, human interactions are reduced thereby weakening the bonds of the social contract. One of the first financial products I learned about

Edifice of Trust

in my banking career was the necessity of Documentary Letters of Credit. Documentary Letters of Credit are bank guarantees that payment will be made if certain documents are presented to the bank (such as invoices and bills of lading, etc.). Documentary Letters of Credit are necessary when importers and exporters do not know each other very well and are worried that the goods will not be delivered or to the contractual specification (assured by the accompanying documents) or that the specified payment will be paid in full and on time (assured by the bank guarantee). It is not that economic transactions cannot be done when there is little or no trust but it does make them more difficult and expensive.

We also want to know that if, in spite of all these efforts to assure trust, things do not turn out well you have recourse to the courts to obtain justice. The assurance that people or institutions that do not live up to their responsibilities or violate the valid laws of the social contract will be subject to the decision of the court (whether compensation, penalties or both) increase the general level of trust in society.

The citizens of the social contract create a government to manage (among other responsibilities like national defense) police powers, civil and criminal courts and the regulation of economic activity. Some of the social issues that afflict our country arise because of the manner government implements these responsibilities. Government is ultimately a human creation being run by humans. It will do well at some things and poorly at others and it will, absolutely, fail from time to time.

We live in an era where many people are asking the government to do more and more. But as government expands into areas outside its core competence, it will likely do a poorer job. What makes a product or service better? Motivation to make profits, competition from other providers and innovation. Government is not driven by any of those motivators of excellence. The progressive political ideology does not like profits, competition or innovation, but especially profits. Karl Marx said that capital derived from profits taken from labor "comes dripping from head to foot, from every pore, with blood and dirt". Progressives believe it. They are wrong. History, economics and psychology have proven Marx wrong at every turn. Government is not the answer to every problem we face and as the Soviet Union and Communist China have proven it is government that can, in fact, be dripping with blood and dirt.

The Role of Regulation by Government

The role of regulation is to foster trust among citizens. Not to press an ideological agenda or squeeze profits out of economic transactions. Proper regulation should increase the volume and fluidity of economic transactions. Increasing trust among citizens increases their confidence in entering into economic transactions and taking risks. Unknown or shifting regulatory environments, costly or burdensome rules and regulation inhibit economic activity.

Good regulation will increase profits. The way to make more profits is by improving products and delivering better services; not from building shoddy products or price gouging. These are not sustainable and are in contravention to the social contract. Proper regulations will hold companies and individuals accountable for these breaches of trust.

Laissez-faire (let it be in French, a concept of commerce free of government interference) does not work well unless all parties to a transaction are fully aware of all the relevant information needed to make a rational decision. This is not feasible in a modern economy even if all the parties are forthright in providing all the relevant information. There is just too much detail. If I read the privacy policy of every website I visited I would have no time to visit websites. Good government regulation can make sure that information provided is not false or misleading, that it is not so fraught with legalese to be intelligible, and that we have legal recourse if necessary. Of course, the laws, rules and regulations need to abide by these principles as well.

The Affordable Care Act (better known as Obamacare) is a regulatory nightmare, especially for smaller companies. But complex regulatory requirements by government are not necessarily a breach of the social contract. But they do violate the contract when they use the coercive power of the state to force companies to provide health insurance to their employees. Company

Edifice of Trust

provided health insurance was traditionally a benefit used to attract employees, not a backdoor mechanism to provide universal health insurance coverage (besides being a very poor means of doing so).

The role of rules and regulations is to make interactions between citizens of the social compact easier and more efficient by increasing the level of trust. This increased level of trust must, of course, be justified by the actions of all parties. Someone who trusts inappropriately is just a sucker and no one likes be taken for a sucker (despite one being born every minute).

The level of regulation in the United States has skyrocketed in the twenty-first century without an accompanying increase in the level of trust due in part to the increasing complexity of the regulations themselves. Increased regulation has done nothing to reduce special tax exemptions, cronyism and favored treatment of elites. When the people see government working for the benefit of special interests they become cynical and lose faith in government.

Trust in Government

In order for the government to be able to provide services that enhance trust among citizens and promote the functioning of the social contract, the people must have trust in the government. There are many factors that relate to trust in the government such as transparency, honesty, accountability, etc. The government must be relatively efficient in the delivery of the services it is required to provide. Broken promises do not build trust (but politicians always promise more than they can deliver).

We are constantly inundated with cartoons and jokes about the government bureaucracy as epitomized by the long lines at the Department of Motor Vehicles. These urban myths are based on fact. A more tragic example is the mess the government has made of healthcare provided for our veterans by the Veterans Administration. The list can go on and on but the point is the government isn't good at doing a lot of things and some of these things can be better managed by the private sector. For example, the government of El Salvador granted a concession to a private sector company to manage the issuance of government ID cards (documento unico de identidad) that was a

Edifice of Trust

roaring success in a region where government bureaucracy and inefficiency puts ours to shame.

Progressives just don't get it. They believe that eliminating profit will reduce the cost of providing a service (through a government monopoly) with no drop off in quality. They don't understand that the profit motive is the incentive to increase competition and innovation that makes products and services better at lower cost.

As the government tries to provide more and more services to the public it just gets larger and more inefficient. In the private sector yesterday's industry giants are today's has-beens. IBM and Yahoo are mere shadows of their former selves as smaller more agile competitors have taken their business. The opposite, in fact, occurs with government services as organizations become more ossified each passing year and enforcement of government edicts becomes more repressive. Why do people want more government when the Pew Research Report indicates that trust in government is near its lowest levels since the **Eisenhower administration**? Beats me!

Worse yet. As trust in government declines and rules and regulations get more restrictive and repressive compliance declines. As compliance declines the government must resort to more and more state power to enforce its edicts. We only have to look to Venezuela to see this lockstep toward greater repression (as presciently predicted by Freidrich Hayek) on fast-forward. The government of President Maduro in Venezuela recently handed over food distribution to the military as the country's starving population ignores the government's rules in a desperate search for food. Think that Venezuela can't happen in the United States? Think again.

The Current Rejection of the Founders Vision

Following the Founders' vision has made America the richest, most powerful country on earth. I cannot for the life of me understand why people are turning their backs on the Founders' vision in favor of an ideology that has seen nothing but failure. The presidential campaigns may cloak their true intentions with patriotic slogans, flag waving and other shenanigans to make us

Edifice of Trust

think they are following a grand tradition of American politics. Both the Democratic and Republican candidates firmly rejected the Founders' Lockean vision of democracy.

We could have, of course, done better. America's history is replete with failures and reprehensible acts. And philosophical idealism will often be pushed aside by common politics. But if we maintain our core principles we have a mark that will guide us toward getting back on course.

The current amalgam of progressive and populist programs boosted by the candidates bear no relation to the founding principles of our nation. Progressive and populist regimes have not only not succeeded, they have often collapsed in spectacular fashion or been subjected to devastating wars of their own making.

Democracy and free markets have brought, not only America, but also the entire world more prosperity than it has ever known. Despite income inequality, people are living longer, less people are starving, fewer babies are dying. Poor people in the United States are richer than most people around the world. They have cars, TVs, smartphones. You want to jeopardize that for regimes from the likes of Stalin, Mao and Chavez? Or the likes of Mussolini, Peron or Berlusconi?

It is true that America has problems and that there are many social issues being debated. The purpose of this book is to show how we can work to resolve these difficult social issues using the principles of the Founding Fathers.

Edifice of Trust

Chapter 3

Race Relations

A Deficit of Trust

I am beginning our discussion on principled resolutions to serious social issues with the issue of race relations. Not because it is the topic of the moment with ongoing protests against police brutality by the protest group Black Lives Matter or because of the spate of recent ambush attacks and murders of police officers which have increased 88% over the previous year. No, I am addressing race relations because it is the longest standing and most intractable social problem dating back to the founding of our country and before.

First a Little Historical Context

Slavery is an ancient (but not honorable) institution. Enslavement of peoples dates back to the dawn of recorded history and probably before. Slavery existed in virtually all ancient cultures. Many of the people of democratic Athens were slaves. Rome was an equal opportunity slaver. Approximately 30-40% of the population of Rome was slaves. Most of Rome's slaves were of European origin. The Muslim Caliphates continually raided sub-Saharan regions to obtain black slaves.

Edifice of Trust

Slavery was spotty in some cultures and endemic in others. Slavery made economic sense in certain geographical locations where slave agricultural labor was effective. The feudal system in medieval Europe that tied peasants to the land they worked was essentially a form of slavery. There were sporadic efforts to eliminate slavery and the slave trade but these were generally ineffective until such time as economic and technological advancements made slavery uneconomical in relation to other forms of labor.

Slavery in America is very much tied to our colonial roots. Slavery on English soil was found unsupported under English Common Law in a famous King's Court case (Somerset v Stewart) in 1772. Despite valiant efforts by the British abolitionist William Wilberforce it was not until 1807 that parliament finally passed a law that abolished slave trading throughout the British Realm (notably North Atlantic slaving), and not until 1832 that Parliament outlawed slavery itself. France banned slavery in 1794. The United States Constitution banned the importation of slaves but only beginning in 1808. And that ban gave slave traders two more decades to bring slaves into America.

Slavery in America was not unique or exceptional in global terms in the eighteenth century. What was unique and exceptional were the words of the Declaration of Independence that stated that all men were created equal despite the fact that approximately 20% of the population of the new nation of the United States was enslaved.

Many of the Founding Fathers and early presidents of the United States were slaveholders. Washington and Jefferson had many slaves. Washington freed his slaves on his death but did not free the slaves of his wife Martha because he felt he did not have the legal authority to do so. Jefferson is said to have fathered several children by his Negro slave, Sally Hemings. Many of the founders seemed equally uncomfortable with the conflict of their stated ideals (to which they had pledged their lives, fortunes and sacred honor) and the legal and the economic necessities of slavery. Plantation farming would have been uneconomic without slave labor (so much for their pledged fortunes).

When it came to drafting the US Constitution, in order to forge a nation, the states of the north and the south had to strike a political compromise on

Edifice of Trust

slavery -- the Three Fifths Compromise of 1787. The Compromise allowed blacks to be counted (partially) but only for purposes of state representation in Congress (otherwise the North would have had a very dominant position in the House of Representatives.

It wasn't until 1863 that President Abraham Lincoln emancipated American slaves, in a civil war that devastated the south and that nearly destroyed the country.

Segregation

Emancipation didn't solve the problems the freed slaves faced. During Reconstruction federal troops enforced laws granting blacks equal rights and access to voting booths. But after federal troops left in the 1870's southern states enacted numerous laws (Jim Crow laws) to preserve racial segregation. These laws required that accommodations, schools and other places where citizens came together be "separate but equal" for blacks and whites. But they rarely were.

In the 1950's, I often visited and actually lived for a while in the South. I remember the white and colored drinking fountains. My cousin and I used to climb up to the balcony of the movie theater, which was reserved for colored people, and throw popcorn down on the (white) people below. That annoyed the people on the main floor and angered (and possibly frightened) the colored folk in the balcony (Back then we didn't call them blacks or African-Americans. They were called Negros or colored people – or worse.).

But segregation is serious business. Segregation made blacks a permanent under-class in America. The laws were designed to keep them down and to prevent their ability to vote. Schools were substandard in order to deny blacks the ability to advance themselves. Prestigious and lucrative job opportunities were not open to them. Sports were blocked to them and black baseball players were relegated to the "Negro Leagues". They were not even able to play themselves in theaters as white minstrels donned blackface to portray colored people. As a kid, I watched Amos 'n' Andy, a television show

Edifice of Trust

about black people. I did not realize until much later that the actors for the Amos and Andy radio show, on which the TV show was based, were whites.

The Civil Rights Era in the 1960's began to change all that, but very slowly (undoubtedly more slowly for blacks than whites). And it has not been easy. Martin Luther King, Medgar Evers, ordinary black and white people, and even little black schoolgirls have paid a price in blood so that blacks could gain the civil rights – in practical terms – that they deserve. It would be easy to say that that's old history – look at the progress that has been made. Really? Look at nine dead churchgoers murdered by a racist white punk in 2015.

After fifty-plus years of civil rights advances white people felt that black people should be happy with the progress they had made. Jackie Robinson broke into the major leagues in 1947. Black athletes have come to dominate many sports, even golf. Black entertainers are prominent although behind the camera they are not as well represented (and let's not talk about the Oscars). We have even elected a black man as president. White people were positively smug about integration and racial harmony. So what happened? Why are race relations near the lowest point since the Eisenhower administration?

Discrimination

Black people still feel that they suffer from discrimination. They have a point. (And a lot of whites feel threatened by black anger.)

I had thought (along with most other white people) that there was much less discrimination today than in the past. Then I watched Senator Tim Scott, a black Republican from South Carolina, get up on the Senate floor and describe the discrimination that he has suffered even while serving as a senator of the country. Among many other indignities, he had been pulled over by police seven times in one year. I haven't been pulled over by police since the nineties.

Senator Scott is a clear-spoken, well-educated man. He has done all the right things to get ahead in the United States and has achieved great success as his reward. Either Senator Scott is a very, very bad driver (unlikely) or black people have a point. More than a point. A grievance.

Edifice of Trust

We have to be careful here. Discrimination is a basic part of human nature. It is one of our vital defense mechanisms. Prehistoric humans needed the ability to differentiate between safety and danger, between beneficial plants and poisonous ones. Early tribesmen had to be able to determine if a person was one of his tribe (safety) or from a different tribe (danger). This us-versus-them differentiation is inherent in all humans. I believe that it lies deep within the instinctive brain. Our instincts react automatically but can be overcome by our rational brain.

It is a small step between discrimination (1. The act of discriminating or distinguishing differences, New World Dictionary of the American Language) and discrimination (3. Showing partiality or prejudice in treatment, Ibid.). A tribesman's lack of trust in strangers results in a very small circle of trust among family members and fellow tribesmen (to ease identification many tribes have distinctive tattoos and facial scarring). This is a major contributor to the chaos we see in the Middle East, for example. There is little trust among the many tribes and religious sects in the region so conflict is inevitable. All of us feel this instinctual reaction. We must employ our rational brain to expand these small circles of trust to include strangers.

Without an expansion of our circle of trust there is no growth of society. Without trust we would be limited to small, backward, tribal communities. The purpose of the social contract is to expand this circle of trust into a larger edifice of trust that includes people outside our familial or tribal bonds.

It is relatively easy to expand the circle of trust to other people who look like we do, who talk like we do, who worship the same god. This would be a rather limited, homogenous structure of trust that could describe some of the nation states in the modern world. It is more difficult to do this with people who look different, who speak another language or worship another god. This larger, more complex and diverse structure of trust requires a unifying set of principles to hold itself together in place of familiar homogenous characteristics.

In order to reduce or eliminate racial discrimination and prejudice (a judgment or opinion formed before the facts are known, ibid.), we need to make a conscious effort to overcome these instinctual tendencies.

Edifice of Trust

It would be easy to label people who have discriminatory tendencies as bad people but you would be falling into the discrimination (definition 3) trap that is the natural reaction of the instinctual brain. Labeling is discrimination (see, it happens automatically).

So, although racial discrimination and prejudice create hot emotions such as anger, shame and fear, the ultimate way to begin to resolve racial division is through a rational process. It will be especially difficult for black people to do this. They are the victims of this history of discrimination, which continues to this day.

Black Lives Matter, New Black Panthers, Nation of Islam

In reaction to centuries of slavery and segregation, many black people have joined fringe groups that reject everything they identify as white. Some, such as the New Black Panthers, want to create a separate black country out of some of the southern states of the United States. But reducing the circle of trust is turning your back on civilization and progress. The only way to move forward is to expand the circle into an edifice of trust.

Is Black Lives Matter a rejection of western civilization? The website for the group has a web page stating "What we Believe" but it is hard to derive specific policies from the very general, positively worded statements. It does however refer to forming a village and rejecting traditional family structure. This would appear to be a reversion to the communalism of an idealized African tribalism.

One of the main themes of this book and of my first book, Principled Policy, is a rejection of tribalism as a type of organization for a modern society. A tribe is not an edifice of trust; it is a hut of trust. It is a relatively small group of people with the same customs, the same language, the same religion. Many of the people in the tribe are related. Tribes were a good mechanism for organizing society in ancient times when peoples of different ethnicities, cultures and religions were relatively isolated from each other. Tribes do not work well in a complex urban society. Professor Scott Page, in his book, The Difference, noted that diverse groups tend to find better solutions because diverse people approach problems in different ways. This is why cities are hotbeds of productivity and innovation. We need to integrate the black community (and other diverse communities) into larger society and not form small pockets of racially or religiously homogenous groups. It will not just be good for these diverse communities. It will be good for all of us.

Reparations

One of the demands of Black Lives matter and other groups is the payment of reparations based on the gains whites have made over many years from the institutions of slavery and segregation.

There are a lot of problems with reparations. First, the people that would be forced to pay the reparations will resist furiously. The onerous reparations imposed on Germany by the Versailles Treaty were one of the primary causes of the rise of Hitler that led to the Second World War. Reparations from the Bosnian Civil War have left that country in political chaos. Reparations are very divisive. You do not get any healing from reparations.

The second problem with reparations is how do you determine who pays the reparations. How about a white person that immigrated to the United States from Poland in 1987? That person wasn't responsible for the harm caused by slavery. My family was in the United States during the time of slavery but I don't know if they owned any slaves or benefitted directly from slavery. How about President Obama? He's half white. Should he have to pay reparations at a discounted rate? Also, should he receive reparations? His black father was from Kenya so President Obama's heritage does not include slavery (he's also done pretty well).

Thirdly, what would be the benefit of reparations to the black community? Twenty two TRILLION in welfare dollars since the War on Poverty began have not sufficed to bring the black community out of poverty. The motivation for reparations is not justice but vengeance.

This brings me to the most important reason that we should not require reparations. Reparations are backward looking and we need forward looking solutions to racial problems in the United States. We need to find a way for blacks and whites to live in harmony as inhabitants of an edifice of trust we call the American Social Contract. If you seek continued racial conflict (and the black community needs to realize that some of their leaders are invested in this) then reparations are the way to go.

Police Brutality

Many in the black community view the police as an armed force of the white elite that is meant to keep black people down. They view the police as the enemy and form neighborhood gangs as a means of protection. Although I do not think this view of the police is accurate it is sometimes hard (and also politically incorrect) to refute their position when confronted with some act of police brutality.

The police force is largely white and made up of officers who do not live in the neighborhoods they police. But according to US government data as quoted by Newsweek Magazine, the number of minority officers has almost doubled since 1987. The largest gain was by Hispanic officers but black officers increased from 9% to 12% of the total number of officers (blacks represent about 12.6% of the total US population). So although minority participation has improved, progress has been better in some communities than others. Watching TV news coverage of several police assassinations in 2016 I noted that the chiefs of police in the Dallas (Metro and Transit) and Baton Rouge were all black.

One of the proximate causes of the recent growth of Black Lives Matter and other protests groups has been a spate of killings of unarmed black men and boys. I don't want to go into the details of each case as this only exacerbates raw emotions. But a striking point has been the trivial nature of the infractions that led up to a lethal reaction. Traffic stops, shoplifting, selling contraband cigarettes. These are minor, petty crimes. There has to be a way to keep these confrontations from escalating (ironically the Dallas Police Department has been recognized as in the forefront of this type of training for officers).

Edifice of Trust

The only explanation I can come up with for this type of overreaction by police is fear. The black community has a higher rate of crime and a higher level of homicides than other communities. Blacks are killed about 4 times as often as whites. Most of the perpetrators of black homicides are other blacks. While black people (primarily men) are more likely to be killed by police than other races, they are also more likely to be committing a crime. The effort by police to reduce crime in black neighborhoods results in more confrontations with black criminals and thus a higher probability that the encounter will escalate.

Edifice of Trust

Reforming the Police and the Courts

Reform the Police
The manner in which the police enforce the law and try to keep the peace in the black community is a flash point that has exacerbated race relations generally.

Quality of Life Enforcement
One might think that quality of life police enforcement (also known as broken windows policing) might resort in a higher level of incarceration. However in New York City, quality of life enforcement (arresting people for misdemeanor infractions such as breaking windows, spray painting graffiti, street vending, trespassing, etc.) actually resulted in a 17% reduction in the prison population from 2000 to 2009 (Time Magazine, 12/17/2014).

The black community should welcome quality of life law enforcement because the quality of life they are promoting is in the poor communities that many blacks inhabit (the quality of life in the suburbs is already okay).

Non-Lethal Weapons
The flash point of recent racial tension has been the killing of black suspects (often unarmed) by police officers. The number of people of all races killed by police in America is very large (statistics are not very reliable but most

estimates are a thousand or more per year). Although most people killed by police are white, the number of black deaths is disproportional.

One disturbing element in some of the recent killings of blacks has been the relative triviality of the nature of the crimes of which they were accused (as noted above). Even if the suspects resist there is little justification for killing someone for a minor traffic stops or the sale of contraband goods.

The police need access to more and better non-lethal alternatives including Tasers and other electromagnetic stun weapons, pepper spray and mace, and sonic weapons for crowd control. There have been protests against the abuse of these weapons but they have been effective in reducing the number of deaths despite their limitations. Expansion of the use of such weapons along with the development of better non-lethal weapons would help ease tension in the black community.

De-escalation Training

Training in deescalating confrontations between police and citizens of all colors is essential. The police motto says it all – to serve and protect. Not to enforce. Police in many countries around the world are viewed as the enforcers of unpopular and unresponsive regimes that are run for the benefit of the elites. America and other western countries are supposed to operate on a different and higher standard. The police, like all public officials, work for the people. It is their obligation to work with citizens to achieve an appropriate outcome even when the citizen is breaking the law.

This may be especially difficult when working with the black community. The black community has a centuries old grievance that has not been fully redressed. When dealing with authority this may cause blacks to act based on these grievances rather than the incident that caused the police response. This could cause black suspects to act more aggressively as if they had a chip on their shoulder. If aggression is met with aggression then confrontation is inevitable. Police need better training in how to deal with these situations.

It may take decades to resolve all the grievances of the black community. De-escalation is not a temporary fix. It needs to become a fixture of police response to the public. Not because they are black, but because they are citizens.

Reform the Court System

There are many black people in prison. In 2014, 6% of all black men were in prison compared to only 1% of whites. A black man has an almost one in three chance of going to prison at some point in his life. That is a staggering number, especially since ex-cons have difficulty finding jobs, voting or getting custody of their children. A prison sentence transforms your life and rarely for the better. As a society we need to find ways of keeping black men out of prison. The question is how to do it without endangering society by letting dangerous criminals loose on the street. The increase in the incarceration rate has been accompanied by a reduction in the crime rate. Any effort to reduce the incarceration rate that resulted in an increase of crime would be rejected by the general public.

Change Mandatory Sentencing

Mandatory sentencing has been blamed for the very high incarceration rate for black men. Many of the offenders had relatively small amounts of drugs when arrested -- often crack cocaine. But penalties for crack cocaine were mush more severe than for other drug offenses such as possession of powder cocaine. Since the threshold for mandatory sentencing for crack was so much lower than for cocaine, many of the prisoners received harsh sentences as if they were pushers rather than users. This harsh treatment fell mostly on the black community.

The rationale for the extra heavy penalties for crack use was an attempt to discourage its use through harsher sentences. But like many well-intentioned laws it had the unintended consequence of jailing young black drug users for many years. The sentencing discrepancies between crack and cocaine have now been reduced but many non-violent drug offenders still languish in jail. Toward the end of his second term in office, President Obama pardoned over 500 hundred of these prisoners.

Edifice of Trust

Reform Education

Education is the only way for the black community to succeed because it is the only way for anybody to succeed. Only a very few people have the raw talent to become a success without education. The ones that do succeed without education are so few in number that they can have virtually no impact in the community at large except to continue the delusion that education is not an important success factor. In fact, a lack of proper education (especially about finances) has left many wealthy athletes bankrupt and destitute after their athletic careers.

Education will be dealt with in more detail later in this book. Here we want to discuss specifically how it impacts the black community. There are several issues that must be addressed so that education can help to improve lives in the black community. Some of these issues affect all kids but others relate directly to black and other poor communities.

Getting Good Grades is not "White"; its Smart

Black kids that get good grades in school are often accused by their peers of "acting white". This is potent medicine. Popularity and getting along in school is extremely important to young kids as they assert their independence from their parents and family. Parents need to reinforce the message of the importance of education. Asian "Tiger Moms" are famous (or infamous) for pushing their kids academically. But Asian kids excel academically as a result.

Edifice of Trust

Black moms need to be "Lionesses" (to use an African big cat) on the education of their children.

Crappy Schools

So what's a black parent gonna do to make sure his or her little kids get a great education if the neighborhood public school is crappy? Black parents need more options than just public schools.

There are a growing number of educational options in the US including charter schools and online public schools such as K12. Results can vary widely so it is vital that adequate standards be established and that these educational options be audited for results.

In the case of black kids and other poor kids, they may lack the ability to take advantage of the opportunities available to them. Teachers' unions try to prevent taxes from funding these alternative educational options. This may require poor people to pay out of their own pocket. In addition, they may lack the home computers and Internet access that is necessary in modern education techniques. We need to develop ways to deliver these kind of technological advancements not only in the schools but at home as well. US corporations that will need skilled workers in the future should step forward to help educate these kids.

Another critical dimension is a home environment where minority students are encouraged to, and given a safe environment in which to do their homework. The family support structure is critical, as are good examples of success through education. Prior to Dr. Ben Carson coming on the stage, where were the positive role models for success through education? (Well there is also Thomas Sowell, Juan Williams and many others but you get my point.)

Graduation Rates

The rate of graduation from high school by black kids trails that of kids of other races. The Journal of Blacks in Higher Education state that only 42 percent of black college students graduate within six years of entering compared to a 62 percent graduation rate for whites. The gap between blacks and whites has been narrowing but slowly. Black women have a much higher graduation rate than black men (46% to 35%).

Affirmative Action

Although Affirmative Action is in contravention of the principle of equality before the law, it is widely supported by the public and by all ethnic groups. But while affirmative action can cite individual success stories, it has not been transformative to the black community. We need to rethink affirmative action so that whatever program we come up with can be an agent of change for black and other poor communities. If Affirmative Action cannot be transformative it will be hard to justify its continuance.

First, we should change the concept from racial preference to a preference to certain levels of poverty. Charles Murray, in his book *Coming Apart: The State of White America 1960-2010*, showed that many of the problems that afflict black communities also afflict other poor communities. It would be inappropriate to create a program intended to lift a people of a certain ethnic identity out of poverty while condemning people of a different racial identity to more generations of poverty.

Even with help in getting into college, future success is not guaranteed. A legacy of crappy schools and cultural indifference to education will hold back kids coming from poor communities. I bet a smart educator could come up with a program to get poor kids ready for college. I would also bet that American corporations would fund a good part of this "boot camp" as well as other aspects of college education.

Gang Culture

In a neighborhood filled with alienated teens that are constantly harassed by police and where unemployment is endemic it would be almost impossible not to have gangs. Gangs offer a sense of belonging and protection (despite the fact that many gang members die young) to young men that have been denied access to mainstream society. You can't get rid of gangs and gang culture through police action. You can only eliminate gangs by eliminating the root causes of gangs.

This will not be an easy task and it will not be accomplished overnight. Even if all the residual prejudice and discrimination of white people were totally eliminated, the gang problem would remain. Black leaders need to focus on the causes of gang culture in order to begin to reduce its impact; lack of education, single-parent families and welfare dependence.

Edifice of Trust

No Simple Solutions

It would be nice if we were able to come up with a simple, quick way to fix race relations in the United States. But there is no easy solution to a two hundred year old grievance that is so fraught with emotion. It is going to take a lot of hard work along with pain and suffering. I include this in my little book, not because I have the solution, but because the solutions offered by politicians are so inadequate.

One candidate offers the iron fist of a law and order crack down and the other offers a gravy train of new goodies paid for by others.

It is important to have law and order but in order to have law and order the people must respect the law. Laws must be reasonable and just. Enforcement must be even handed. In the Philippines, President Rodrigo Duterte has plunged the country into a horror of vigilante justice by declaring open season on drug pushers and telling police that he will not prosecute them from killing drug dealers. In the first month of Duterte's administration between 300 and 500 suspected drug dealers (or innocent people accused for other reasons) were executed by vigilante death squads. That is not the rule of law. It is lawless rule.

Progressives, on the other hand, believe you can solve problems by giving people things. But free stuff cannot fill the hole in the heart of the black community. Taking money from wealthy people (or future generations) to give to poor people of all races doesn't engender self-respect, it engenders obligation (which is what the progressives hope is true when it comes time to

Edifice of Trust

vote). A government handout can't give a person self-respect: that comes from earning a decent living by your own accomplishments.

To integrate the black community into the American edifice of trust will take tremendous effort from both blacks and whites. I had thought we were getting close but apparently we still have a long way to go. The millennial generation seems less occupied with racial differences (as well as many other differences) than my generation and I know from experience my generation is more tolerant than my parents'. Despite our current problems we are making progress. We must stay the course.

Chapter 4

Changing Demographics

Diversity vs. Consensus

The demographic profile of the United States is changing. The population is aging and is becoming more diverse. Immigration has had a large impact on this changing demographic structure.

As recently as 1910, 89% of the people in the United States were white. Blacks were a little less than 11%. Other ethnic groups were lost in rounding errors. One hundred years later whites were only 72% of the population (64% if you don't count white Hispanics). The percentage of blacks in the population increased slightly to almost 13% but the blacks were eclipsed by Hispanics who increased to around 16% if you include white Hispanics. Asians went from rounding errors to 5%.

In 1948 90% of Americans said they were Christian. That number has now fallen to 70% due, in large part, to a large increase in the number of people who say they have no religious affiliation. There is a large number of other religions whose numbers are increasing substantially but each represents a small portion of the population. The percentage of Jews in the population has fallen from around 4% to around 2%.

Edifice of Trust

The Population of the United States is also aging. The number of people over 65 is expected to increase substantially as baby boomers pass that milestone. This increase is not just in absolute numbers but also as a percentage of the population. This fact has tremendous fiscal, as well as social, implications.

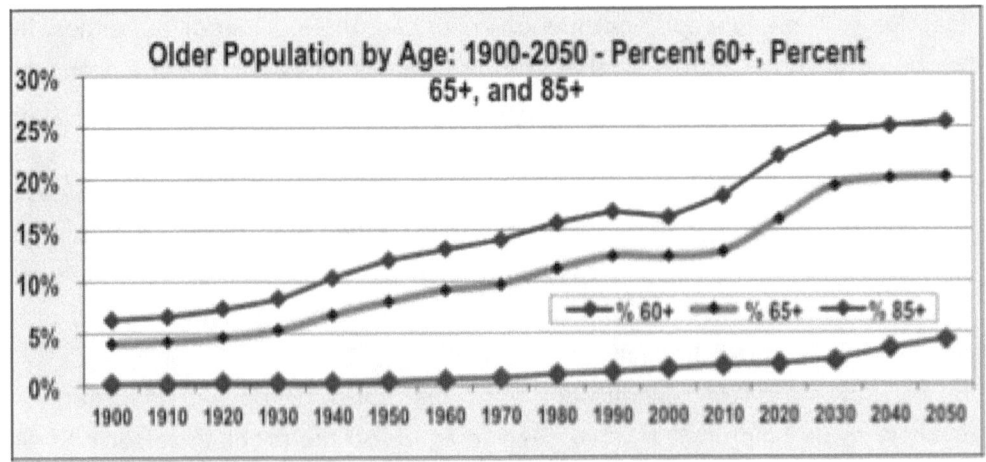

Source: Department of Health and Human Services

The question is: how will these demographic changes affect the American Social Contract? We are currently seeing our country morph from a free market republic toward a European-style welfare state. Could it be due, at least in part, to the large influx of immigrants from eastern and southern Europe in the decades prior to World War One? They were accustomed to centralized monarchical regimes such as the Austro-Hungarian Empire, the kingdoms of Italy and Spain, and the Prussian dominated German Empire and Czarist Russia. Of course, they were fleeing those oppressive regimes but it is still an interesting speculation.

The popularity of the 2016 presidential campaign of socialist Senator Bernard Sanders shows how far we veered from the visions of the Founders. Democrats are attempting to take advantage of recent immigration flows by recruiting Hispanics to their left-wing causes (although why Hispanics would flee heavily centralized governments of elites to vote for one here in America is beyond me).

The Benefits of Diversity

Professor Scott Page, in his book *The Difference*, explains how complex adaptive systems function and how diversity can obtain superior outcomes. In the book he shows how a diverse group of people can outperform a group of experts. The people in the diverse group will view the problem to be solved in different ways. They will try various approaches to solving the problem and often come up with the best answer. The group of experts can solve an easy question in a snap, but if it is a real head-scratcher they might be stumped. Why? Because, being experts, they were probably all educated the same way and will approach the problem in the same way. If the problem stumped one expert it might stump them all.

But there are several conditions that must be applied in order for diversity to be helpful. First, they need to agree on the problem to solve. If all the diverse people in our group seek to solve different problems the outcome may be less than optimal (which is another way of saying disastrous). Another condition is that the people in the group have some understanding of the problem. If it is a scientific problem, combining a physicist with an engineer, a biologist and a mathematician might be a very productive combination. Adding a beautician probably would not be very helpful (although the beautician might be helpful on a different problem).

The United States has greatly benefitted from its diversity. Although one could say that, prior to WWI, that it was primarily a "black and white" nation as indicated above, the whites came from many different nations in Europe and from many different cultural traditions (and cuisines). The blacks as well came from many different tribes and kingdoms. The United States was much more diverse than any country in Europe at the time.

Edifice of Trust

<u>The Benefits of Consensus</u>
Many people have been upset, nay distraught, about the gridlock in Washington. Our diverse nation is seeking solutions to different problems. The result is less than optimal. The conservatives/Republicans seek to solve one set of problems while the progressives/Democrats try to solve different ones. The conservatives/Republicans try to solve the fiscal and economic problems facing our country while ignoring the impact of these policies on social problems. Progressive/Democrats try to solve social problems while ignoring the impact of their policies on the budget and the economy.

I believe that our conservative/progressive/Republican/Democratic politicians cannot agree on policies because they have lost sight of what unites us. We are not a nation of accountants or a nation of victims. I have always been drawn to the poem of Carl Sandburg ever since I first heard it as a boy in Chicago.

> *Hog Butcher for the World,*
> *Tool Maker, Stacker of Wheat,*
> *Player with Railroads and the Nation's Freight Handler;*
> *Stormy, husky, brawling,*
> *City of the Big Shoulders:*

This, to me, embodies the spirit of America: rough-hewn but hard working. Sandburg goes on in his poem to list the flaws of the great city but follows this with the pride he feels for the city accepting both the greatness and the flaws.

America is a lot like that. Not accountant but hog butcher. Not victim but toolmaker. Of course the hogs we butcher are genetically modified and the tools we now make are in hypertext. The world has changed since Sandburg penned his poem and America with it. But it was not the jobs and actions but the spirit that Sandburg described in his poem. It was that spirit that made America the most powerful country in the world.

Edifice of Trust

What the Founders envisioned was a nation where the citizens were unencumbered by government. "Unencumbered" does not mean there was no government. It means that the government did not hold its citizens down. That government facilitated peoples' freedom and their ability to pursue happiness.

In a diverse nation we need shared goals so that we are trying to achieve the same objective. That way our diversity works for us. If we allow our diversity to send us all over the place trying to pursue diverse objectives then we will achieve nothing. Government is not the answer and no government is not the answer. Government is a tool (one of many) that we use to achieve our objectives. We need the right tool because many of our tools can be harmful as well as beneficial. Fire was essential for primitive humans develop a society that evolved into a civilization. But fire can burn us or kill us or destroy all the things we have created. The same can be said for nuclear energy. Harnessed it can provide bountiful energy. Unharnessed it provide the greatest destructive power we have ever known. The same can be said about government.

<u>The Serendipitous Conjunction of Diversity and Consensus</u>

There can be no agreement on how to use this tool of government if we do not have a consensus about what we want to achieve. I assert that what we should want to achieve is freedom. The freedom to pursue the goals and objectives that each of us may have as long as we do not interfere with others that are also pursuing their own objectives. This means the economic and political freedom of all people. The role of government is to promote the freedom of the people while ensuring that the rights of others are not infringed. In order to accomplish this we have ceded certain powers to the federal government by means of the US Constitution. Our unifying principles should be the ones established by the Founders: a republican form of democracy (note lower case r) personal liberty, economic freedom, equality of opportunity, the rule of law and equality before the law. Many of the rights guaranteed in the Constitution, such as freedom of speech or freedom of religion, are derivative of these basic principles.

Edifice of Trust

Once we frame our search for solutions to social problems within these principles we can use our diversity to seek out optimal solutions. That does not mean the solutions are easy. Sometimes they can be horribly difficult. It took a bloody Civil War to end the abuse of slavery and even that did not resolve the problems of discrimination and segregation that faced the black community. A problem we are still working to resolve to this very day.

But America has been veering away from our founding principles even as politicians erect a new leviathan of government while pontificating about American values. American principles are based on the theory of government expounded by John Locke in his *Second Treatise on Government*. The people cede a certain amount of their liberty to empower the government such as the power to impose taxes in order to fund the operations of government. But as Benjamin Franklin warned, those "who can give up essential liberty to obtain a little temporary safety deserve neither liberty nor safety." In order to receive the safety of welfare checks, healthcare benefits and other "entitlements" we have been ceding our essential liberty. Welfare checks and other "free" stuff from government (actually taxpayers or future generations) don't make people free. It makes them dependent. It breaks their spirit. It makes them a permanent under class.

A majority of the people in this country believes that we are going down the wrong path. Yet they keep electing people who only promise to take them further down this same path, heading further into the wilderness. Our politicians are like Professor Page's group of experts. There is no diversity in their thinking. They just keep trying the same old thing over and over again. We need a fresh perspective. But it is not a new perspective but the Founders perspective. If the Founders were alive today, how would they view the world? How would they view America?

<u>Immigration, Diversity and Consensus</u>

People have been immigrating to America ever since it was discovered. It was the Land of Opportunity. Initially they were primarily from Northern Europe, especially Great Britain. They brought with them not only their Christian religion and traditions but also the theory and practice of government. Their home countries still had kings but they also often had parliaments and local governments were relatively independent. For the colonists, communication with the authorities back in England took months so naturally they had to exercise their independent judgment. Even with royal governors the colonists often took matters into their own hands.

As noted above, later immigrants came from Central, Eastern and Southern European countries where civil authority was placed in the hands of monarchical governments. There was no local independence in many of these countries. These immigrants fled the conditions in their mother countries while others stayed, so clearly they were outliers. America was in the process of maturing as a nation. Did America change them, or did they change America? Or a bit of both?

The concept of the welfare state, first developed in Imperial Germany under Bismarck, now predominates the European continent. One of the motivators of the Brexit vote was a reaction to the overwhelming bureaucratic oppression of that ever-growing super-state. But even as the mounting troubles of this growing monstrosity appears to have reached its limit of super high taxes and increasing deficits, many progressives, such as Paul Krugman, look to the European Union as the ideal form of government. Did these immigrants bring with them the seeds of the destruction not only of their governments but also of ours?

The Impact of Immigration

It is an interesting question. Has wave after wave of immigration caused America to shift away from Lockean democracy and move toward a Hobbesian welfare state? Or is this move a natural progression? In 2016, the Trump campaign and many of its supporters obviously thought so. At his campaign rallies, he proposed building a wall on the southern border. One of his first acts as president was to block (at least temporarily) the immigration of Muslims from the Middle East.

Edifice of Trust

In the second half of the twentieth century new waves of immigrants began entering the United States from south of the border, first from Mexico and then many other countries from Latin America and the Caribbean. Latin culture is much more hierarchical than American culture. Orders come from the top and work their way down the hierarchical ladder. In one ministry of finance where I was working as an advisor, I was having a problem with one of my counterparts who wasn't doing the things we had agreed upon. Finally I had to go around him and talk to his boss. I was reluctant to do so. In American business culture going behind someone's back is not a good thing to do, so I expected some blowback from my counterpart. Instead, he thanked me. By going to his boss I had relieved my counterpart of the responsibility I was trying to get him to undertake. It was now his boss's problem.

I have always said that the immigrants from Latin American countries are among the best those countries have to offer. Immigrants are outliers. Unsatisfied with the state of things in their home country they pull up stakes and leave. Immigrants, especially illegal immigrants, are risk takers, willing to bet on their ability to face an uncertain future. Of course there are rapists and murderers among these immigrants, but there are rapists and murderers in any large population of people. Sure Latin gangs seem to be able to cross the border at will but remember that Latin gangs are a US export to the region. MS-13 and Mara Salvatrucha started in LA (that's Los Angeles not Latin America) not in El Salvador.

And Latinos are hard workers. In Latin America they often have to commute two hours each way (often walking because there is little public transportation) to get to their poor paying jobs. In the US, Latino immigrants do the work that others do not want to do. They work hard, they save and they start small businesses. By the second generation many are living the American dream. Why they would vote for the progressive agenda of the Democratic Party is beyond me. George W. Bush got about 44% of the Hispanic vote in 2004. Mr. Trump only got 29% in 2016.

Democracy also does not fit comfortably in many Asian cultures where authoritarian models predominate. Democracy is flourishing in Japan and Korea

Edifice of Trust

but people in Hong Kong are finding, that, in the case of the promised one China two systems, both systems originate in Beijing. That Asians gravitate toward a Hobbesian style leviathan is not surprising as they are comfortable with that style of government. They are, however, high tech and entrepreneurial so one would think that they would prefer a Lockean system but most high tech entrepreneurs support the progressive agenda (which is very surprising to me except for the case of Elon Musk).

Islam is not only a religion but also an ideology. Many of the basic tenets of Islam conflict with those expressed in the US Constitution and western culture in general. This could potentially make their integration into the American Social Contract more difficult. The American Social Contract places the free expression of one's religion in a special position that the state cannot inhibit and also prohibits the state from establishing a particular religion or squiring religious tests for office. This prohibition of government interference allowed many religions to flourish in the United States in an era where many countries had an official state religion. State religions are pretty much a thing of the past except in Islamic countries. Toleration of other religions in Islamic countries waxes and wanes depending on the civil administration or the interpretation of religious texts. Other religions may be tolerated but their adherents are not permitted its free expression. Many Islamic countries prohibit the formation of Christian churches, erecting crosses or religious celebrations such as Christmas lights. A poll conducted by the Polling Company found that 51% of Muslims in America favor sharia law over that of the US Constitution (note: readers need to be advised that the Polling Company was founded by Kellyanne Conway who is a senior advisor for President Trump. An in-depth poll by Pew Research neglected to ask that question). Muslims are, as yet, a very small minority in the US (around 1%) but Islam is the fastest growing religion in the world. As such they are unlikely to have a very profound impact, positive or negative, on the American Social Contract but there could be a looming confrontation between these two cultures on the world stage at some point of time in the future.

Edifice of Trust

Conclusion

It would be a stretch to blame immigration for the shift toward Hobbesian progressivism but it might have been a contributing factor. But uncontrolled immigration can change the nature of a country. Just ask the Celts who were the previous inhabitants of (now Anglo-Saxon) Britain. Europe is in the throes of a desperate wave of immigration of people fleeing violence and poverty in the Middle East and North Africa that is disrupting civil society across the continent. As part of the European Union, Europeans accepted some internal migration in exchange for the economic benefits of open internal borders. But as waves of Middle Eastern and African refugees pore into Greece and Italy they have spread rapidly across the continent. Many believe that the Brexit vote was motivated by the desire to close the border to these immigrants.

The number of refugees that the US has agreed to accept is unlikely to cause much disruption here but there are legitimate security concerns. As a humanitarian gesture, the US accepted about 70,000 Somali refugees back in the 90's. A number of them (or their American born offspring) have returned to join Al Shabaad or ISIS.

Each wave of immigrants had to go through a process in order to become Americans. They arrived here knowing little about America. Only that it was a golden land of opportunity. They may not have known much American history or even English but they knew one thing. They wanted to be Americans.

New immigrants are being seduced with a progressive vision that America is a giant welfare state, a grab bag of healthcare benefits, welfare checks, high minimum wages and endless retirement funding. That isn't the America our ancestors came to be a part of. That isn't the America that Carl Sandberg described. But it can be. We need to get back to the Founders' original vision. Then with all our diverse group of people we can achieve Professor Page's optimal results.

Edifice of Trust

A Principled Immigration Policy

Immigration policy was a key issue for the 2016 election and will be an important element in the domestic policies of the Trump administration. President Trump is following up on his campaign promise to build a wall (and have Mexico pay for it) although at the time of writing construction has not started. This statement, no matter how impractical it might be, resonated with a large swath of the population. Further, he stated that he would deport all the non-documented immigrants although he later back-pedaled on that commitment. Mrs. Clinton, on the other hand, wanted to grant amnesty to undocumented immigrants and allow them to become US citizens despite having broken the laws of the United States to come here. She would also encourage additional immigration. The positions of the two campaigns and their political parties is firmly entwined with the perception that most of these immigrants will vote Democratic once they become citizens.

But politics is, by definition, unprincipled. So how are we to come up with a principled immigration policy without the taint of politics? It is trite to say that America is a nation of immigrants. Trite, but true. But that would apply to most countries if you go far enough back in history (or prehistory). Human populations move. They have done so ever since they made their exodus out of Africa. Boundaries have been fought over. Boundaries move as a result of war. Civilizations rise and fall. A country that cannot protect and maintain its boundaries will soon cease to exist.

Edifice of Trust

Most countries in the past and the civilizations they represent have been ethnically and religiously homogenous. Large-scale migrations of ethnically and religiously different people have been forcibly resisted or have resulted in the demise of that civilization and its replacement by a new civilization.[2] America is ethnically and religiously diverse by traditional standards. The binding force holding America together has been its Western, Enlightenment culture and civilization. Although founded initially on traditional European culture and the Christian religion it has advanced to a point where it can accommodate people of multiple cultures and religions.

An immigration policy that attempted to maintain the American identity by restricting immigration to white Christian ethnicities would not be in keeping with our principles (although there are many people that would prefer exactly such a policy). Conservatives want to freeze us in a nineteenth century vision that would be like a diorama in a history museum. But a principled based policy that strived to maintain our American uniqueness and exceptionalism is not only justified, it is essential.

Progressives would sacrifice American principles on the altar of multiculturalism. Progressives want to turn us from our Lockean principles of personal liberty and economic freedom toward a Hobbesian communal leviathan led by an intellectual elite. One of the levers they intend to use to accomplish this goal is through open borders and multiculturalism. These policies are not based on the American Founding Principles; they are intended to overthrow them.

The United States has gone through several rounds of immigration reforms and attempted reforms. Each effort has foundered on the problem of what to do about undocumented immigrants already in the country, who number in the many millions. Any proposed reform will have to deal with not only the existing undocumented immigrants but also those who will attempt to

---

2. The Chinese appear to be an exception to this rule. For example the Mongols conquered China in 1271 but were gradually overwhelmed by Chinese culture and a population that far outnumbered the invaders.
India as well has been able to survive multiple invasions and takeovers.

come after. These efforts have often failed on the fact the children of these undocumented immigrants that are born in the United States are considered US citizens by birth. Any effort to deport illegals is faced with a Hobson's choice of separating families or deporting US citizens.

This dilemma is created by the concept, known as birth right citizenship, that anyone born on US soil is a citizen. The 14th Amendment (1868) to the US Constitution states:

"All persons born or naturalized in the United States, and subject to the jurisdiction thereof, are citizens of the United States and of the State wherein they reside."

The intent of this clause was to guarantee that the slaves recently freed after the Civil War were citizens of the United States. It was not intended to apply to the children of people illegally or temporarily in the United States. It has, however, been generally considered that any child born in the United States (or its overseas installations such as army bases) is a US citizen. While this does not automatically grant citizen rights to the illegal parents, it does make it much more difficult to deport the parents. The legality of birth right citizen citizenship for illegal aliens or tourists has not been legally challenged. The United States and Canada are the only developed nations to grant birth right citizenship[3].

A principled reform to current immigrations law would be a law that:

1. Places restrictions on birth right citizenship as applied to undocumented immigrants, tourists and other temporary visitors. This clause would likely be challenged and would likely require a Supreme Court decision.

---

3. Of course, the United States should base its decision on principles and not what other nations do. But it is interesting that our progressive friends are pushing birth right citizenship while their European social democratic paradises don't. Ah, politics!)

Edifice of Trust

Too bad that the Court has become so highly politicized that a principled decision is unlikely.

2. Provides funding to strengthen border security. Reliance on a wall is futile. The two thousand mile long border between the US and Mexico is dwarfed by our twelve thousand mile coastline. All the tens of thousands of refugees from the Middle East and Africa are flooding into Europe via the Mediterranean Sea. We must be smarter in developing ways to stop illegal crossings.

3. Develops methods to track the people who over stay the time limits of their legal visa (such as tourists and students).

4. Develop a temporary worker program similar to the Bracero program (but without the civil rights abuses that plagued that program).

5. More strictly enforces immigration rules on companies hiring foreign workers (there will always be people who will try and operate off the books but we can make it a lot harder for them to do so).

6. Structures the citizenship test to require a more in-depth understanding of the United States than the current test that can be memorized in an afternoon (it would be a good idea to test our high school students as well so that they understand the responsibilities they are gaining when they become adults). Test should be in English only.

7. Deports illegal aliens that are criminals (this is a no brainer).

8. Creates a new class of temporary resident visa specifically for undocumented immigrants currently residing in the US (most other temporary visas are for people planning to come to the US – i.e., legal unless they overstay). We can call these cards yellow cards as compared to green cards. Yellow cards presume that residence in the US is temporary and that the visitor will ultimately return to his or her own country. The children of yellow cardholders will not automatically be granted birthright citizenship. After 10 years as resident in good standing, yellow cardholders can apply for permanent resident status (green card). Once in possession of a green card they can begin the process of becoming an American citizen.

Edifice of Trust

The reality we face is different than the one President Trump is selling. Most illegal immigrants crossing our southern border are not Mexicans looking to take American jobs. More Mexicans are returning to Mexico than are coming in. These immigrants are refugees fleeing the violence of the Central American drug wars created by the American War on Drugs. The front line of that war is in the Northern triangle of countries (Honduras, Guatemala and El Salvador). If we want to stop this flow of refugees we need to stop this crazy war and give them a modicum of peace and security.

The other immigration quandary we are facing is the flow of refugees from the Middle East. During the campaign, President Trump wanted to ban the immigration of all Muslims but was roundly excoriated for this notion. But Muslims do pose a problem. Some of their coreligionists are opposed to western civilization and are waging a terroristic war against what they view as a decadent and oppressive civilization (of which America is the most prominent member). The Charter of Medina decreed by Muhammad states that the main binding tie of Muslims is religion over blood kinship (their tribes and by extension the nation state). So Muslims living in the west are conflicted, do they support their country or the Ummah (the community of Muslims)? I asked some Muslim friends how they relegated this seeming irreconcilable difference. They assured me of their love for America and all it represents and suggested that for theological interpretation I speak to a religious scholar. There are, of course, majority Muslim countries that are secular. But Egypt's experience with the Muslim Brotherhood and Turkey's current drift toward Islamization highlight this inherent conflict. The plight of refugees from the Mideast conflicts is heartbreaking. But the Islamic State has declared its intention to secrete combatants within the ranks of these refugees (some of which have made attacks in Europe). Extreme caution must be taken.

A principled immigration policy deals with immigrants compassionately and especially in the case of refugees. But a principled policy must also guard those very principles that are the foundation of our social contract. Because we are multiethnic, multi religious, diverse country anybody in the world can become an American citizen and join in our social contract. But because being

Edifice of Trust

an American is not based on ethnicity or religion doesn't mean that just anybody off the street can be an American. Americans believe (and will fight and die to defend) our American Founding Principles.

Chapter 5

Gender as a Political Tool

LGBTQ (let me know if I should add some additional letters) Issues

In this modern age with our improving (but not yet perfect) understanding of how the human body functions, I don't understand why issues related to people with sexual dysphoria should be a political issue rather than a medical or psychological one. Although sexual dysphoria of all types have traditionally or religiously been labeled perverted and evil, it is becoming increasingly clear that the vast majority of the people in these communities experience sexual dysfunction not of their choosing. The human body and brain are complex and subject to a wide variety of conditions. When other parts of the body are formed differently than the accepted standard, the medical community rallies to understand the problem and to see what can be done. But when it comes to sexual differences everybody gets all worked up about them, blaming the individual rather than genetics, evolution or other factors that could be the cause.

Edifice of Trust

Evolution wouldn't exist if all living things didn't suffer from genetic mutations and adaptions. Darwin figured out over a hundred years ago that certain genetic changes would favor the adaptability of a creature to its environment and that individuals with that characteristic would thrive, survive and reproduce. The corollary to this theory is that genetic changes that proved unsuitable resulted in the death of the individual animal without reproducing offspring to continue the mutation. Most of these evolutionary experiments do not succeed and those traits are consigned to a genetic dustbin. Human sexuality being one of the most complex aspects of our humanity, it is not surprising that genetic mutation, chemical imbalance and other factors not yet discovered cause a wide variation in sexual identity.

<u>Male Homosexuality</u>
Homosexuals are not willful miscreants, immoral satyrs or straying sinners (well they could be that regardless of the condition of homosexuality). We do not know the definitive cause of homosexuality (more likely multiple causes) but we do know that homosexuals are made that way. They cannot stop being a homosexual and convert to heterosexuality. MRI scans show that the brains of homosexuals are different from those of heterosexual men and more similar to those of heterosexual women. Scientists cannot at this time determine if the brain differences caused homosexuality or if homosexuality caused the brain differences. However the causality is irrelevant because the bottom line is that homosexuals cannot control their sexual orientation. So while I may be a bit queasy contemplating sex with another man, a homosexual would likely feel equally queasy about sex with a woman.

But there is another aspect of homosexuality that makes me wonder. Darwinian evolutionary theory would say that because homosexuals reproduce less often that this trait should become extinct in the human species. Nevertheless, homosexuality is well documented in ancient writings and is known to exist in all cultures and ethnic groups (although more suppressed in some than others). We can only speculate about prehistory but bonobos (genetically very similar to modern humans) are known to engage in homosexual activity, which would lead us to believe that it existed in human prehistory as well.

But why does homosexuality continue to exist? It does not fit the Darwinian mode of survival of the fittest. Or does it?

Despite recent efforts to put homosexuality into the mainstream, homosexuals are different from heterosexuals. Not just in sexual preferences but in other ways as well. Homosexuals are disproportionally represented in many intellectual and artistic areas. Professor Scott Page asserts in his book, <u>The Difference</u>, that a diversity of viewpoints will obtain superior results. He goes as far as to state that a heterogeneous group of non-experts (in this case, a heterogeneous group made up of both homo- and heterosexuals as well as other diverse individuals) can outperform a homogeneous group of experts. Could it be that homosexuals provide the human species a competitive advantage by offering a different perspective on things?

Whatever the reason for the existence and persistence of homosexuality, it is undoubted that they do exist. And based on Professors Page's studies, societies that embrace homosexuals and bring them in to the edifice of trust that is the social contract are benefitted from their participation. It would be a denial of the principles of the American Social Contract to restrict their access to all the rights of their fellow citizens.

Lesbianism

Lesbianism appears to be a bit different from male homosexuality but recent studies are pointing to genetic or hormonal reasons for the same sex attraction. Causality is important because if lesbianism or homosexuality was just a lifestyle choice then a culture could be justified in saying that a certain type of activity is not acceptable behavior in that culture. Cultures say a lot of activities are not acceptable behavior (some more than others). But if it is caused by genetic, hormonal or other factors the individual is not making a choice but rather is just being who she is. In our American Social Contract, citizens retain their natural rights except in the cases of (i) those ceded to the federal government in the Constitution (or to the states in the state constitutions) and (ii) in instances where the exercise of a person's rights interferes with the rights of another person. Engaging in consensual lesbian or homosexual activity does not interfere with other peoples' rights nor the rights of other people in the LGBTQ community, and so should not be prohibited.

<u>Same-Sex Marriage</u>

Conservatives foam at the mouth that same-sex marriage is ruining traditional marriage and the family. Despite their opposition same-sex marriage has been gaining traction across the country. There has been a sea change in public opinion on the acceptability of same-sex marriage going from 57% opposed (vs. 37% in favor) in 2001 to only 35% opposed versus 55% in favor in 2015. Conservative tradition has fallen to scientific evidence and cultural change. Many religions still condemn homosexuality and lesbianism and reject the concept of same-sex marriage, and that is their right. But their right to their opinion does not extend into the public arena where the other person's rights must be taken into account.

The Founding Fathers would have been flabbergasted at the concept of same-sex marriage but that does not mean that they would be opposed to it. Many of the Founding Fathers had active sexual lives and not always in the conventionally accepted way; Hamilton has an affair with the wife of a rival, Jefferson had children with a Negro slave and Franklin was a notorious womanizer. The Constitution makes no mention of marriage out of the belief that it was none of the business of the federal government. And so it should remain.

I personally don't understand this push to have same-sex marriage. If the value of the homosexual community to the larger society is in their difference, why would they want to engage in heterosexual rituals in order to gain acceptance? There are a couple of issues that arise out of the decision to approve same-sex marriage.

Edifice of Trust

Polygamy and other Arrangements

If a man and a woman can get married, and if two men can get married and if two women can get married why couldn't a man and three women get married? Islam permits polygamy. And so did Mormonism until forced to stop the practice (some Mormon sects still have polygamy). And would not the rights of the individuals involved work in both directions? If a man could have three wives why couldn't a woman have three husbands? Or two men, three wives? You see where I am going with this.

If all the parties agree, why should the government get involved at all? The state is not the guardian of our culture. It is the guardian of the social contract. We are the guardians of our culture and there is no one to blame for our changing culture than ourselves. It is very dangerous to put government in charge of our formulating culture. I would, however, put a few conditions on the practice in order to protect the rights of all involved. The agreement should be in the form of a contract similar to a partnership agreement in business. All parties must be able to enter into a contract. Minors would not be allowed (in some of the Mormon sects the wives were minors married to older men). All parties to the agreement must agree (in other words a man couldn't marry a second woman if the first wife did not agree).

These arrangements would cause some initial consternation. But given the difficulty I (and many other people) have in managing one spouse I doubt that this would be a very common arrangement except among some religious communities. In accordance with the words and intent of the first Amendment Muslim families would have the right to marry as their religions permits. Once the initial controversy died down it would cease to be an issue.

Rights of Children

The rights to all these varied relationships (same-sex marriage, polygamy, etc.) are based on the assumption that no one else's rights have been affected. There has been very little study of the effect of these arrangements on children. If it were proven that these varied marriage contracts were adversely affecting the children of these arrangements, then the state would have an interest in the children (similar to child protective services) and the obligation under the Social Contract to intervene. [4]

Scientists are beginning to closely study the impact of these arrangements on children; but it will take many years before any conclusions could be drawn.

<u>Bathrooms</u>

One of the very early executive orders signed by President Trump reversed an executive order signed by president Obama ordering schools to allow children to use the bathroom of their gender identity rather than their gender at birth. Several states are going even further by requiring that people use the bathroom of their birth gender. This has sparked outrage in the progressive community and their celebrity supporters. Artists and athletes are refusing to attend events in states that have passed such laws (the NBA moved its all-star game from Charlotte because of the North Carolina bathroom bill).

But there is a real tragic story underneath all the headlines and bitter political battles. Our sexual proclivities are not solely determined by what is between our legs. Many other parts of our bodies are involved, especially our brain. It is easy for wires to get crossed and for things to get screwed up. These should be medical issues not political footballs. The science on transgender people is at square one. There is some evidence that there is a biological basis for transgender identity but the causality is uncertain. Certain features in the brains of transgender people were more similar to their identified sex than their birth sex. These features became more pronounced after sex change operations, which would lead one to think that the brain was reacting to something going on somewhere else in the body.

---

4. There have been a number of studies done on the effects of growing up in a homosexual or lesbian household. These studies often show divergent results that are promoted by advocates or opponents of same-sex relationships. The effects I noted, to the extent they existed, were relatively mild and no worse than non-traditional relationships such as single-motherhood. More study needs to be done by impartial scientists, but I don't think they are going to find much.

Edifice of Trust

But the political issue is not how to truly help transgender people but who gets to use which bathroom. Transgender people are very vulnerable and are subject to more bullying and abuse than almost anyone else. Having to use a public bathroom puts them (as well as other people) in a very vulnerable position.

Transgender people and their advocates want them to be able to use the bathroom of their gender identity and not the gender they were assigned at birth. But other people might be uncomfortable with sharing a bathroom with a transgender person. I wouldn't be real happy to be in a bathroom with either Caitlyn Jenner or Chaz Bono.

The bathroom issue is a divisive problem that is not easily solved. People opposed to letting transgender people choose which bathroom to use will be called bad people and anything they say against the transgender bathroom choice will be labeled hate speech. But civil rights are not based on how nice a person you are. They are based on your natural rights as described in the Declaration of Independence. Even nasty people have rights (so long as they don't infringe on the rights of others).

So which side should prevail, the large majority of people who are being asked to give up their privacy rights or the very small minority who may be subjected to abuse when using the bathroom of their birth sex? The transgender community has framed the argument as either/or. No alternatives such as genderless bathrooms or "students' use the nurse's office" are acceptable. Not even the option of creating a third genderless bathroom option in all buildings open to the public (similar to the Americans with Disabilities Act and which would have an enormous expense) is acceptable. Only the transgender advocates' position is acceptable and President Obama agreed and ordered that schools follow suit. President Trump disagreed and reversed his order. But the issue remains unresolved.

This is not a way to build trust. This is a difficult problem that requires dialogue.

Edifice of Trust

Weddings

Now that same sex marriage has the Supreme Court seal of approval and many people are taking advantage of this new found right, the last line of defense for the religious conservatives (and people who just don't like it and feign religious conviction) is to refuse to provide services to same sex couples that want to get married. There was the famous case of the country clerk in Louisville Kentucky who refused to issue marriage licenses to same sex couples citing her religious beliefs. There was a lot of controversy but as an elected official she could not be fired. A federal judge ruled her in contempt of his ruling that she comply with the Supreme Court ruling. Whether they agree with the Supreme Court's ruling or not, a public official must comply with lawful orders or face the consequences. She was jailed for several days but ultimately relented by allowing the deputy clerk to issue the same-sex licenses. This was not a same-sex marriage issue. The issue here was whether elected officials must follow the rule of law. They must. There is no religious exemption for obeying the law. If you want to change the laws there are ways to do so in a democratic society. But good luck with that since a majority of people now supports same sex marriage.

Then there are cases of providers of services to weddings (such as photographers, pastry chefs and floral arrangers) who choose to not provide their services to same sex couples. They cite their religious beliefs in order to circumvent non-discrimination laws. I say let them discriminate. Only require them to publish their intentions prominently on their web page and shop windows. That way, same-sex couples (and their supporters and anyone else who doesn't like discrimination) can deny them their business. Given the support for same-sex marriage by the public, these service providers are likely to lose a lot more business than just same-sex couples.

The Uncertain Future

Doctors and scientists in the future will be able to manipulate genes and biological functions to heal the human body and to protect future generations from life threatening diseases. These same techniques have the ability to affect or change human sexuality. Already in India people are using sonograms to determine the sex of a fetus and then only bringing the boys to term. If the Russian government establishes an elaborate scheme for doping athletes in order to win Olympic medals what makes you think they will hesitate to try and make genetically enhanced athletes in the future? (Better check their junior athletes right now!)

The LGBTQ communities are already marrying and having or adopting babies. Would they want children that had the same sexual orientation that they have? I don't know. But in the future this option will be available. Would parents who knew their unborn baby had Down syndrome permit genetic alteration to prevent such an occurrence? Would it be ethical? Would it be such an ethical leap to alter the sexual orientation of unborn babies?

I ask these questions because there are still forces of nature that we do not fully understand. Is there a reason that sexual dysphoria continues to exist in spite of Darwin's survival of the fittest? Does sexual dysphoria give human beings a competitive advantage over other species? Does a relatively small number of differently oriented individuals give us enough diversity to obtain the superior results as Professor Page's theory suggests? Would too many of these individuals skew diversity in the wrong direction? Luckily we don't have to find the answer to these questions right now. But we will one day.

Edifice of Trust

The War on Women

The phrase "War on Women" has been trotted out by Democrats and other progressives to describe the Republican Party's policies that affect women. This is typical of progressives who try to portray people that oppose their policy proposals as bad people. There are, of course, bad people in the Republican Party. Just as there are bad people in the Democratic Party. And in government. And in business. And in every other human endeavor.

They are trying to dull your critical thinking ability by reducing all the complexities of issues relating to women to a bumper sticker. Don't be fooled. We can discuss the issues relating to women in a reasoned and rational manner without having to think of one side as a bunch of evil, misogynistic Neanderthals (or the other side as a bunch of bull dyke harpies).

Women's issues fall into three broad categories; reproductive rights, violence against women, and workplace discrimination. (Voting and property rights were granted over a century ago.)

Reproductive Rights

Although there are many nuances regarding the issue of reproductive rights, all the arguments boil down to two things: who is going to pay for healthcare costs relating to women's health and when does a fetus become a human being.

First let me say that the healthcare system in the United States is all screwed up. It is screwed up for everybody, not just women.

Edifice of Trust

Back in the good ol' days, health insurance functioned like real insurance. People paid out of their own pockets for routine health expenses like doctor visits and treatment for non-life threatening diseases. Health insurance covered major medical expenses like an accident, major disease or the birth of a baby. When I was young and healthy I had a major medical policy with a very high deductible. I didn't need coverage for little things but I wanted to make sure I was covered in case something major happened to me. When I got my first job after graduate school I also got a healthcare benefit (medical and dental) as part of my compensation package. The company that hired me offered the benefit voluntarily in order to make their offer of employment more attractive. There was no government compulsion.

There was, however, a government provided incentive for companies to provide health insurance. My company could deduct the cost of my healthcare benefits (in essence part of my salary) but I was not taxed on the value of the benefit. Companies used to provide many benefits to top employees like memberships at country clubs and company cars but the IRS slowly squeezed those perquisites by taxing them out of existence. But not healthcare. That stayed.

The legislators that passed the law providing the double tax exemption probably thought they were doing a good thing. Everything was wonderful back in the good ol' days. But then some people got to thinking, why should I pay the routine medical expenses with my after tax salary instead of through the company provided insurance. It made economic sense. I could get more medical benefits without having to pay taxes while the company could deduct the costs of giving me more benefits. The company could shift the structure of my compensation to more benefits and less salary. I would be better off because my compensation package would stay the same but I would pay less taxes. The company's costs would stay the same.

So more and more procedures were included in the coverage and deductibles were reduced. When my daughter was born 80% of the costs of the delivery were covered by the insurance and I paid 20%. There were some complications in her delivery that increased the total cost. That would have

Edifice of Trust

been difficult for me to pay completely, but because the insurance covered 80% I was okay. Also, a critical dimension was that when I paid 20% out of my own pocket, I was personally involved in the decision of what medical services to buy, and where the trade-off was between "must have" and "can do without" health services. 80/20 company plans went the way of the dodo. Thank you Mr. Taxpayer for paying the cost of my increased medical coverage.

You are probably wondering what all this has to do with the War on Women. Wait, wait! I am getting there but you need to know the larger issue in order to understand the details.

Because of the advantageous tax treatment more and more companies began to offer expanded healthcare benefits (we will get to the unintended consequences later). In addition, healthcare benefits covered by insurance expanded to cover virtually every expense: checkups, well baby visits, you name it. This is not insurance. When you buy insurance for your car what are you covering? The unexpected cost of an accident. You don't use car insurance for an oil change or a new set of tires. Insurance covers unexpected expenses. Not so, health "insurance". It covers everything.

But not everybody has this health "insurance". Many low wage jobs did not include healthcare coverage. Part time work usually does not include healthcare coverage. More and more people are now working as independent contractors who are not considered employees and therefore not entitled to benefits.

The Affordable Care Act (Obamacare) has now made healthcare benefits mandatory with a detailed list of what procedures are covered (there are no government regulations that are not accompanied by miles and miles of red tape). Much of the War on Women is about what is covered and who pays for it.

In my book, *Principled Policy*, I advocate an elimination of the double tax exemption for healthcare expenses and the elimination of the mandated coverage required by Obamacare. These are the first steps toward getting government out of the healthcare industry and letting the free market economic system do its wonders as it has with much of the rest of the economy.

Edifice of Trust

With the elimination of this government interference in the market, it is hoped that consumers will take greater responsibility for their healthcare and how it is paid for. The competitive forces that drove 60" flat panel TVs from $5000 to $500 will work their magic on healthcare.

In 2012 the issue was who should pay for women's birth control medicine. Perish the thought that a woman desiring to purchase her discretionary birth control medicine must actually pay for it. Obamacare made sure that birth control medications were covered under its plan and to make sure that the insurance pool was large enough to reduce the overall cost for these medications, men were also included. So men not wanting to pay higher premiums for insurance coverage for birth control meds they will never need (unless they go through a sex change operation) is translated into a war on women.

If we can solve the healthcare problems of the double tax exemption, the employer mandate and other problems created by Obamacare much of the War on Women falls away. Men and women would be able to select insurance policies that meet their needs, not the government's. Religious organizations and companies with religious owners would not be forced to provide coverage that they are religiously opposed to because they would not have to provide coverage at all. This is not a war on women. It is the freeing of men and women to make their own healthcare decisions.

Abortion

And then there's abortion. Abortion is not a pecuniary issue but a social, moral and ethical one. Cost is not relevant here (although many people oppose paying for something they consider not just wrong, but murder).

Abortion rights appear to be the Holy Grail of progressive women. They want unrestrictive access to all forms of abortion at any stage of pregnancy for any reason for all women and girls. And they want the taxpayer to pay for it. It is now easier for a fourteen-year-old girl to get an abortion than any other medical procedures (all of which would require at least parental approval).

Edifice of Trust

I can understand the transformational effect an abortion would have on a young girl, pregnant and unmarried. The life of a young single mother is very hard. It is difficult to finish high school let alone attend college. An abortion could change that girl's life in a big way for the better, in many ways.

Abortion is also transformational for the fetus, and not in a good way. Progressives like to frame the abortion issue about the woman's right to choose. But, argue the pro-life advocates, what about the fetus' right to choose? This is the ethical question we have to ask. At what point does an unborn baby get the right to choose (or have a presumptive right to choose to live)? Is it only after live birth? Could it be some time prior to live birth? The tenets of faith in many religions include the sanctity of life from conception. That life is a gift from God and is holy. Genetics shows us the fetus has a unique set of chromosomes at conception. But, although many people have deeply held religious beliefs about abortion, we cannot look only to religion for our answer.

Under the principles of the American Social Contract an individual's rights are almost unlimited unless they infringe on the rights of another person. If a person wanted to amputate their little finger they would have the right to do so (unless judged mentally unfit, which would probably be the case). But a finger does not have the potential to become a human being.

Some data on Abortion

To understand the potential impact of a change in abortion policy, it is necessary to look at the data on abortion in the United States. In this brief overview, it is not a question of which policy option is good and which policy option is bad. Both policy options are bad. We are faced with a choice of deciding which is less bad.

The good news is that the rate of abortions is going down and, especially, the rate of teen pregnancies and abortions are down substantially from their peak. Here's the bad news. The Guttmacher Institute states that there were 1.06 million abortions in the United States in 2015. That means over a million women answered the ethical dilemma of unwanted pregnancy by aborting the fetus.

Edifice of Trust

Here is what Health and Human Services said about this issue.

"The national teen pregnancy rate has declined almost continuously over the last two decades. The teen pregnancy rate includes pregnancies that end in a live birth, as well as those that end in abortion or miscarriage (fetal loss). Between 1990 and 2010 (the most recent year for which data are available), the teen pregnancy rate declined by 51 percent--from 116.9 to 57.4 pregnancies per 1,000 teen girls. According to recent national data, this decline is due to the combination of an increased percentage of adolescents who are waiting to have sexual intercourse and the increased use of contraceptives by teens.

The rate of abortions among adolescents is the lowest since abortion was legalized in 1973 and 66 percent lower than its peak in 1988."

That is some good news. We are heading in the right direction. But the Guttmacher Institute also noted that between 1973 and 2011 there were almost 53 million abortions in the US. The US population in 2011 was 312 million. If all those aborted babies had lived the US population would be 17% larger (actually much larger because many of those babies would have had babies in the course of 38 years). What are the implications for our labor force? For the make-up of the population? For immigration policy? 53 million means it's a big issue.

<u>Could it be the Supremes got it right?</u>
There is no solution (with current technology) that could possibly appease the two opposing advocate groups. They are both dealing in absolutes and no compromise on their positions is possible.

Gallup polls dating back to 1975 indicated very consistent results showing that approximately half of the US population support abortion under certain circumstances. About 30 percent of the population support abortion under any circumstances while about twenty percent opposes abortion under all circumstances. So while those that oppose abortion may have the correct ethical and theological position they lose politically. There is a strong, consistent opinion held by the US public that abortion should be allowed in some or all cases.

We have just seen in the Chapter on Race Relations that the rule of law is dependent on the reasonableness of the law and the support of the general population for the law. A ban on abortion would not meet this test. However, only a minority (which has been fairly consistent over time) supports an unrestricted right to abortion.

The Supreme Court addressed the issue of abortion in 1973 and issued an opinion (Roe v. Wade) that has been under fire ever since. That decision stated that once the fetus was viable (able to live outside the womb –generally assumed to be about 21 weeks) the state had a legitimate interest in the potential life. This ruling allowed abortion prior to viability but allowed the state (the individual 50 states in this case) to regulate or restrict abortion after viability. The ruling has been roundly criticized for creating rights not addressed in the Constitution but it remains the law of the land. Anti-abortion advocates continue to have the states further restrict abortion but the Supreme Court recently (June 2016) rejected a Texas law they deemed too restrictive.

Moving Forward

If we assume that abortion is bad (but not as bad as millions of unwanted pregnancies or as bad as young women getting dangerous illegal abortions) then we must find other ways to reduce abortions within the law that will be supported by population.

The trends, as noted above, are encouraging. The rate of unwanted pregnancies among teens has dropped to record lows, perhaps because of sex education in public schools. The rate, however, remains high among poor and minority women. Education about preventing unwanted pregnancies and the availability of birth control medications would help further reduce the necessity of abortions. Progressives would say this is the job of government but I would counter that this is the job of the Pro-Lifers and other women's groups that want to reduce unwanted pregnancies.

Edifice of Trust

Likewise, if pro-life groups wanted to reduce the number of abortions they should promote adoption services to women and girls who might have difficulty in placing a child that they are not able to support for whatever reason.

Violence Against Women

There is no doubt that the safety of women is a critical part of the social contract. No one condones violence against women (or anyone else, for that matter). But when progressives talk about actions to end or reduce violence against women they are talking about programs and laws that they hope will help the situation. But when conservatives oppose these proposed programs the progressives shout that the conservatives hate women and are waging a war on women. From the conservatives' point of view the progressives are waging a war on the budget.

You see, all these new laws and programs require money. Money from the government's budget, i.e. the taxpayer and/or future generations (in the case of public debt). Progressives say, "how can you sacrifice women's safety in order to balance the budget?" They say that about all the myriad of laws and proposals they push for all the victims in the country (which, to progressives, is just about everybody but white men). But budgets aren't limitless and the government has many other priorities that must be balanced with benefits provided to citizens from all sorts of programs.

Women's advocates, government and other people that are opposed to violence against women need to review all these programs to determine which are effective and can serve women best within national budget limitations.

Workplace Discrimination - The Wage Gap

One of the other issues that progressives like to use to further divide the country is the so-called wage gap between the pay of men and women. They like to reduce a complex situation (which may or may not be a problem) to a single statistic, as if this statistic provides all the explanations needed. Women make on average 82% of what men make on average.

Edifice of Trust

The question we must ask is how does the wage difference between men and women (assuming there is one) affect the level of trust in the social contract? Progressives point to an inequality of outcomes to suggest that women should not rely on the system of the social contract to protect their interests. But the social contract does not guarantee equality of outcomes; it guarantees equality of opportunity. The question we must therefore ask is, "do women have the same equality of opportunity as men when it comes to earning a wage in the United States?" A follow-up question would be, "can unequal outcomes be explained by factors other than discrimination?"

Historically women have been subjected to tremendous level of discrimination not just in America but just about everywhere in the world. Women were treated as property in many ancient societies and even in some countries in recent times. Some religions relegate women to an inferior status. Even in democracies women had to fight to get the right to vote. Women in the United States got the right to vote less than one hundred years ago. In 1950, only about a third of women were in the labor force. In 2015 it was over 60% (men's participation was over 70%). Traditionally women were relegated to women's jobs: female secretaries to male managers, female nurses to male doctors, etc.

Women have made a lot of progress in the last hundred years. Yet there are some that say that this progress has been insufficient by pointing to a persistent (although declining) wage gap between men and women. Significantly, the Bureau of Labor Statistics' report on women in the workforce which noted the 18% wage gap added a caveat to its report on the gap saying "the comparisons of earnings in this report are on a broad level and do not control for many factors that may be important in explaining earnings differences".

Women still tend to gravitate to "female" professions such as nursing and education that are relatively low pay. In business men will seek out manufacturing or finance jobs (high pay) while women will tend toward Human Resources (relatively low pay). I would just like to point out that during my 40-

Edifice of Trust

year financial career I have had many female bosses (who I assume made more than I did).

But women and men are different. A study by Ransom and Oaxaca (2005) showed that men had a significantly higher elasticity in the supply of labor than women. This means, after all the economic formulas that you have to pay men more to get them to stay on the job. Men demand raises and leave when they don't get them. Women hope for raises, and tend to stay more.

According to Pew Research, the wage gap is much reduced in the millennial age cohort (women earning 93% of their male counterparts). This could mean that in the future the wage gap will cease to be useful as a divisive issue. It also means that using state power to force an outcome preferred by progressives but not justified by rational analysis would cause inequities of its own, thereby undermining the edifice of trust.

Edifice of Trust

Comment

Women and people with sexual dysphoria have real, legitimate issues that need to be addressed. The question isn't if but how. Solutions need to respect the rights of everyone while addressing the needs of these communities. Unfortunately, advocates of these causes and their progressive allies are often not interested in solutions. They will not accept anything but absolute surrender from those who resist their proposals. Absolute surrender may be the ideal outcome of a war but it does nothing to build an edifice of trust.

Of course, the leaders of these rights advocates groups and progressives are dedicated to the continuance of these divisive issues, not their resolution. Their livelihoods depend on the continuance of the fight, not a peaceful end. A true solution will address the needs of the people, not the demands of the advocates.

Of course, advocates opposed to increasing the rights to the LGBTQ community and religious leaders opposed to abortion along with their conservative allies are invested in their fights as well. The pollsters and the media are complicit in these fights, framing their questions or coverage in simplistic terms. I refuse to take polls because I don't think they ask the right questions (like presidential polls that don't include the choice of "none of the above").

Framing issues in simplistic black and white positions and demanding absolutist resolutions will lead to nothing beneficial (except the continuing

Edifice of Trust

lucrative salaries of the advocates). Only by framing the issues within the concept of the American Social Contract and its underlying principles can we build the trust necessary to truly resolve these issues.

The trends on most gender issues are moving in a principled direction, including more people within the edifice of trust that is the American Social Contract. Conservative positions not based on the founding principles are losing support of the American public. Some issues (such as the children of same-sex couples) still need more study to determine what the principled position should be.

The principal issue not moving toward resolution is the issue of abortion. Although the trends are moving in the right direction (fewer abortions) public opinion has been steadfast in its support of at least limited abortion. From our 21st century perspective many of the things our ancestors did were abhorrent, things such as slavery, treating women as chattel, laws against sodomy, and others too numerous to name. It makes me (and perhaps you) wonder what future generations will think of us and our tolerance of (and even promotion of) abortion.

Edifice of Trust

Chapter 6

Foreign Trade and Employment

Foreign Trade and Employment

Foreign Trade (specifically the trade deficit) was a principal issue in the 2016 campaign, not because of its economic impact, but rather its impact on employment. Even more specifically, the trade deficit's impact on good, blue-collar jobs.

The 2016 presidential campaign was the first campaign where the candidates of both major parties have attacked free trade, vowing to abort the Trans-Pacific Partnership deal and renegotiate the North American Free Trade Agreement (NAFTA).

Mr. Trump claims that NAFTA is a disaster (should I say disasta, it would rhyme). It is true that in 1993, just as President (Bill) Clinton was signing NAFTA, the US had a trade surplus with Mexico of $1.7 billion. In 2015, the trade deficit was $60.7 billion. To Mr. Trump that is losing big time. But in the 22 years since NAFTA was signed, US exports to Mexico have increased 5.6 times from $41.9 billion dollars to $235.7 billion dollars. Discounting for inflation trade in goods increased 3.4 times. The US export of services has increased 193% since and has a surplus of over $9 billion. Some people might say that was winning big time.

Edifice of Trust

It is true that Mexican exports to us increased even more, from $39.9 billion to $296.4 billion, thus the large trade deficit. That increase in trade created many new jobs in Mexico, some of which were lost by people in the US. But US exports also created new jobs, many more than those that were lost to Mexico. That is the nature of international trade. It benefits both countries.

It is true that Mexico benefitted more than the US. But Mexico was a poor country and those exports had a big impact on their economy. In 2015, US exports to Mexico represented 1.3% of our economic output. In Mexico, their exports to us represented 25.9% of their output. So while Mr. Trump might consider gaining modestly compared to gaining enormously as losing, I consider it a win/win situation. Foreign trade should always be a win/win rather than a win/lose situation. And for every Mexican with a good job in Mexico there is one less person tempted to swim over the Rio Grande in order to seek a job in the US. Besides, more Mexicans are leaving the US than are coming in. The flood of immigrants that are crossing our borders come from Honduras and El Salvador and other countries.

The big issue for the 2016 election was what to do with the Trans-Pacific Partnership (TTP). One of the first actions President Trump took after his inauguration was to cancel the TTP. The TTP was intended to be a trade agreement between 12 countries around the Pacific Rim and was actually an expansion of a successfully operating trade deal between Singapore, Brunei, New Zealand and Chile. I don't know all the details of TTP and don't want to know (I read portions of the CAFTA-DR deal and know that it is extremely detailed and excruciatingly boring). There are a lot of complaints from various special interests that hated the deal across all the countries. But that's sort of the point about trade deals. Manufacturers love high tariffs that reduce competition and allow them to raise prices. Farmers love closed markets for their products. Everybody loves barriers to trade that protect their profit margins or their jobs. The whole goal of trade deals is to reduce barriers and subject companies and workers to competition.[5] But TTP was more than just a

---

5. That is fine for normal consumer goods. But strategic goods – weapons technologies, intelligence gathering, strategic materials and

trade deal. It was the economic component binding Pacific Rim countries together to better resist the inroads of the rising regional hegemon – China.

And then there's China

In the same 22 years that Mexico's exports to the US grew by 643%, China's exports to the US grew by 1432%. US exports to China have also grown but not nearly as much. China follows a mercantilist trade policy compared to our free trade policy. Mercantilism[6] was popular in the early days of the modern era but most countries have discovered that ultimately it limits their growth prospects compared to the freer trade we promote through trade deals.

China was a pitifully poor (but dangerous) country until Deng Xiaoping began to open up China's economy after the death of Mao. We tolerated their mercantilist practices because we felt that as China became wealthier, it would become more moderate and more integrated into the economic system. At this state of its development China has become the second largest economy in the world but it has not become more moderate and it has not integrated into the world economic system.

Mr. Trump has a point. China is a serial currency manipulator that has thrown up tariff and non-tariff barriers to US (and everybody else's) exports and investments. It has flagrantly stolen our intellectual property. It uses its economic power to threaten its neighbors and corrupt the governments of its trading partners. Its huge population has seduced many multinational corporations but non-tariff barriers have blocked many companies from competing effectively against domestic companies (as Uber recently found out).

---

other such items represent a different issue. These goods do not act subject to solely economic conditions. In times of conflict they can be embargoed or blockaded, leaving a country at greater risk. Most countries keep strategic goods out of trade deals.

6. **Mercantilism** was an economic theory and practice, dominant in modernized parts of Europe during the 16th to the 18th century, that promoted governmental regulation of a nation's economy for the purpose of augmenting state power at the expense of rival national powers. Wikipedia

Edifice of Trust

But Mr. Trump's remedies are provocative and dangerous. If you try and screw China they are not going to take you to the International Court of Justice or the Permanent Court of Arbitration (China refuses to recognize that court's decision on the South China Sea). The US already has a number of trade disputes with China being reviewed by the World Trade Organization. The WTO can allow the US and other increase tariffs within the rules of the WTO as compensation for China's trade violations. The US must continue to pursue prosecuting these and many other trade violations aggressively. This may appear to be too tepid a response but it is a start.

China's trading partners and Asian neighbors are getting increasingly worried about China. They are looking to the US for leadership. Trade deals like the TPP would have helped cement our relations with these countries and reduce the influence of China.

Import Substitution

I grew up in Michigan in the 60's and 70's and back then everybody knew to never buy a Ford or Chevy made in September or October (deer season) or on a Friday. The assembly line was depleted during those times but who cared if the cars were poorly made? But that was before the Japanese and their cars arrived. Today we look back at that blue-collar wonderland with longing for a lost golden time. But that post-WWII era was due to the coming together of a number of unique factors for a brief time that didn't exist before and haven't reoccurred since. The world has moved on and the United States has moved along with it.

When I first went overseas, most of Latin America followed an import substitution economic strategy. High tariffs blocked foreign goods and favored domestic products. But domestic products were expensive and of poor quality. On the advice of my friends I bought my Sony TV in the Tepito market for smuggled goods in downtown Mexico City. I couldn't afford to buy a Sony TV at the department store and the local merchandise was crappy.

Economic policy in Mexico at that time also pushed a strong peso (another form of "winning" and a source of national pride). Normally a strong

Edifice of Trust

currency would favor imports but the high tariffs blocked the cheaper goods. Desperately needed capital flowed out of Mexico. Everybody borrowed in dollars. This house of cards collapsed in 1982 and ushered in the Lost Decade, not only for Mexico but also for much of the rest of Latin America.

This disastrous policy is exactly what Mr. Trump has been advocating. Mrs. Clinton, driven to the left by the success of the presidential campaign of Mr. Sanders, abandoned the support of TTP she advocated as Secretary of State and came out against it. Socialists don't like international trade. Trade is driven by competition and profit. These motivations are anathema to socialists. They reek of exploitation of the workers. The old Soviet Union followed a policy of autarky (economic independence) where economic inputs came from within the country (very similar to import substitution), at a high cost to productivity and competitiveness[7]. International trade is very difficult to put in a five-year plan.

The Illusion of Bringing Back Good Manufacturing Jobs

Both campaigns asserted that they would bring good manufacturing jobs back to America. Both campaigns offered a combination of enticement and coercion (the old carrot and stick approach) to get companies to "re-shore" manufacturing to America.

If it makes economic sense to bring manufacturing back to the United States, companies will do it. The way to make the economics of reopening a manufacturing plant feasible is to use technology to be able to maintain your competitive advantage through increased worker productivity.

A report by Lindsey Oldenski of the Petersen Institute for International Economics stated:

---

7. An interesting insight into this problem was looking at the USSR's aircraft production process. Everything needed to produce a passenger plane was located at a single enormous plant: fuselage, wings, electronics, landing gear, upholstery, seats, etc. all produced in a single plant because they could not rely on parts being shipped to the assembly plant from other places. It was also hobbled by the fact that they had no cost accounting systems in place to track the value of what any producer made.

Edifice of Trust

"US manufacturing employment, both in absolute levels and as a share of total US employment, was falling long before the recent rise in offshoring began. Some of this decline is due to changing demand as US consumers shift their spending away from manufactured goods toward services. However, the largest factor is technological change, which has automated many basic manufacturing procedures and reduced the amount of labor required to produce many goods. In particular, technology is now a substitute for the most routine activities that can be easily performed by machines, and these activities are concentrated in middle and low-end manufacturing (Acemoglu and Autor 2011)."

A recent study by Jan de Loecker and Allan Collard-Wexler of Microeconomic Insights noted:

"While employment in the steel sector fell by a factor of five, shipments of steel products in 2005 reached the level of the early 1960s. Thus, output per worker grew by a factor of five, while total factor productivity increased by 38%. This makes the steel sector one of the fastest growing manufacturing industries over the last three decades, behind only the computer software and equipment industries......This left the industry with only 100,000 workers in 2002 compared with about 500,000 in 1972."

Blue-collar workers with a high school education don't run these new plants, technicians and programmers with a post-secondary education do. President Mr. Trump's promises to bring back the good ol' days of American manufacturing will come to nought unless they do the hard work of preparing US workers for the twenty-first century. Otherwise they will only increase HB1 visas.

Disruption and Employment
Technological change has been destroying traditional jobs and creating new jobs ever since the beginning of the Industrial Revolution. This process of

Edifice of Trust

"creative destruction" was described by Joseph A. Schumpeter in his seminal book, <u>Capitalism, Socialism and Democracy</u>. Creative destruction is an essential part of the free market system. The current buzzword on the business news stations is disruption. All the new tech companies want to disrupt markets and create new market conditions advantageous for their business ventures. Uber is a disruptor. AirBnB is a disrupter. Google, which completely revolutionized the advertising industry, is constantly re-inventing itself so it can continue to be a disrupter. And we are just at the start of 3-D printing, which promises to be an enormously disruptive technology.

Disruption screws up five-year plans, which is why socialists and progressives are against competition and innovation. Disruption screws up traditional jobs, which is why medallion taxi drivers are trying to block Uber politically (because they can't compete economically). If the goal to Make America Great Again is to bring back our industrial glory days then President Trump must think again. If he thinks that government programs (even with the bully pulpit) can contain this disruptive force he must think again. That train has already left the station.

But if you think about it, leaving the station is what progress is all about. America didn't become great by doing things the old fashioned way. Alexis de Tocqueville noted America's unique role as a disruptor in his book, *Democracy in America* (of course he didn't use the word disruptor – it wasn't in vogue then). America has been disrupting the world politically and economically ever since it's founding. If you want to make America great again then you need to make America more disruptive again.

It takes more than tax policies and new regulations to unleash this disruptive force. What the candidates should be focusing on is how to make our youth and unemployed workers capable of participating in this new, highly technical market. They need to come up with policies that will help make our companies more adaptive and flexible. They will need employees with the skills to match the changing economic environment.

Edifice of Trust

With computer technology and artificial intelligence, jobs that can be filled by poorly educated, poorly motivated workers will disappear. Unemployment benefits and welfare checks are not drivers of economic growth. In order to get the US growing at a three percent, four percent or even five percent rate, we need make America Disruptive Again. President Trump needs to come up with way to reignite the American innovation machine and not rely on outdated formulas that are proven failures.

Increasing Employment

In order to create more employment, we need to increase economic growth. The anemic growth we have seen since the Great Recession is insufficient to create the kind of jobs people are seeking. For all its quantitative easing and near-zero interest rates, the Federal Reserve is incapable of boosting employment (if you read <u>Principled Policy</u> you would know why).

The Federal government is a puny employer. Wal-Mart employs almost as many people as the Federal Government. Federal government employment has risen only 8.7% since 1962 (from 2.515 million to 2.733 million in 2014 according to OPM). That's an average of less than two-tenths of one percent (0.17%) per year. State and local government employ a lot more, almost twenty million (a little over half in education). But the level of state and local government workers has actually declined about a half-percent in the last ten years. So government employment isn't the answer to the ever-increasing demand for more (and better) jobs.

It is the private sector that provides the most jobs and almost all of the increase in employment. International trade plays an important role in employment as does tax policy and the regulatory burden. But the most potent force to increase employment is innovation. The candidates need to come up with proposals on how to unleash this potent force.

President Trump has proposed a $ 1 trillion investment in infrastructure over the next ten years (he had to one-up Mrs. Clinton's proposal of a $275 billion infrastructure program over five years) in order to employ many thousands. But that's chicken feed. The American Society of Civil Engineers says that we need $3.6 trillion of investment in the next four years. Think about this. Arcadis, a Dutch consultancy group, estimates the US public and private infrastructure at around $37 trillion. At President Trump's proposed $100 billion a year investment it would take 370 years to replace our existing infrastructure. We, of course, need infrastructure and a lot of it. But keep in mind the fact that while construction of infrastructure does employ many people the goal is not employment but infrastructure to support economic growth. Once constructed infrastructure itself is not a strong source of jobs. You must keep in mind however, that while a lack of infrastructure can impede economic growth, infrastructure itself cannot drive growth. Build it and they will come only works in Hollywood movies. We need real infrastructure not make-work infrastructure.

One way that government can help foster the innovation that drives growth is through funding advanced research in the sciences (even though there is a potential for abuse). The Defense Advanced Research Project Agency (DARPA) has been a wellspring of innovation (the Internet was originally a DARPA project, as have been unmanned aerial vehicles and many other "goodies"). The government can also fund prizes similar to the Ansari XPRIZE for suborbital spaceflight in order to motivate people to achieve goals deemed worthy. There are a lot of innovative ways that government can foster innovation. Maybe we can create an XPRIZE for that.

Smart Regulation

Mrs. Clinton wanted to impose a whole new level of rules and regulations on business while President Trump has stated he will wipe out 75% of regulations. They are both wrong.

Increasing rules and regulations to punish one-percenters for the last recession and to prevent future recessions (an impossibility) will not unleash economic growth. A complex web of regulations is strangling companies and especially small businesses and compliance costs (passed on to consumers) are skyrocketing. But their wholesale elimination can prove to be counterproductive as well. These candidates don't understand the role of regulation in the American Social Contract.

Regulation is supposed to build the people's trust that the social contract is functioning properly. It is the cement that holds the Edifice of Trust together. People want to know that the food is safe, that their banks are well capitalized and that the books of publicly held companies are accurate. But companies shouldn't be audited by the IRS to make sure they are paying for worker healthcare under the Affordable Care Act. The IRS should stick to auditing companies to assure they are paying their taxes, not complying with the ideological orders from Washington.

But a plan to cut regulations to reach an arbitrary figure (that happened to be a campaign promise) also does not make sense. The social contract is not based on laissez faire economics where the burden is on the consumer to have sufficient information to make an intelligent economic decision. Given the plethora of products on a typical grocery store shelf, it is virtually impossible to know what the ingredients are or if they are safe. Do you know what disodium inosinate is and if it is safe? Well it is in your can of Dinty Moore beef stew (of course you wouldn't even know that it was in the can if the government didn't require Hormel Foods LLC to divulge the ingredients). The little logo that says, "inspected and passed by department of agriculture," gives the consumer confidence to purchase the product.

Smart regulation helps to build trust. Minimum capital requirements for banks plus the requirement of deposit insurance give people confidence in the banking system. Inspection by the Agriculture Department gives consumers confidence in their food purchases. These types of regulatory requirements boost economic activity. This is the role that regulation is meant to play in the economy. The Obama administration used its regulatory powers to force companies and individuals to comply with its ideological agenda. This is not the purpose of government and this will not make the Edifice of Trust stronger.

Edifice of Trust

Chapter 7

Education: The Path To Opportunity

The Path To Opportunity

I have to admit that I am not much of an expert on education but given the mess the experts have created I am willing to give it a shot. Its also probably President Trump picked Betsy DeVos to be his education secretary. The Democratic Party (at the behest of the teachers' unions) fought tooth and nail to keep her from being confirmed. She doesn't have the education mindset inculcated into education professionals by the education establishment. She does not accept the poor academic achievement of US students and is willing to try new things to solve this critical problem.

Education is an essential element to achieve the equality of opportunity that is the basis of the American Social Contract. Without education entire swaths of our country could be condemned to second-class citizenship. Because government is charged with maintaining the social contract, government clearly has a role in fostering the education of the people. But what is that role and what measures should government employ in order to fulfill this obligation?

Further, we are in the midst of a technological revolution that puts a premium on education in science, technology, engineering and math (STEM).

Edifice of Trust

Even further than that, this technological revolution is coming at a time of increasing globalization where other nations are challenging America's advantages in technological development and innovation. In the past, it was difficult for countries to develop the industrial infrastructure to challenge a major power. But development today can leapfrog older technologies such as in Kenya where banking inclusion has jumped over the development of bank branches to banking by cellphone (something we are just beginning to get here in the US). It is now more difficult for developed economies to maintain their competitive advantage.

In America we need to make sure that the next generation is well and properly educated not only for the well being of the social contract but for national security. If it comes to war, the next one will be fought with AI (artificial intelligence), cyber attacks and drones. We need the skills to maintain our technological advantage to assure our national survival.

A Nostalgic Look Back/The Traditional Role of Government

Traditionally, education is the United States has been a local affair. When over 90% of people were small farmers, education was the responsibility of parents or the local community. The federal government had no control over local education because it had no constitutional mandate to do so (except the vague "promote the general welfare") and also, in the early days of the Republic, it did not have the capability to provide such services across such a large country.

So education in the United States developed locally and often rurally across the country, which has resulted in our distinctive structure and school calendar. School districts are local and in many areas independent of other forms of local government. School board members are often elected and have their own taxing authority. The initial result was the highly literate populace (for the time) that is necessary for a fully functioning democracy. De Tocqueville was amazed at the high level of literacy of early America and the rampant political discourse and discussion of national events he found as he toured the country. Newspapers and political pamphlets were widely available throughout America and eagerly devoured (this was why Benjamin Franklin wanted to be the first Postmaster General - to promote the sending of pamphlets and newspapers though the mail during the Revolutionary War). This was very different from Europe at the time, where the majority of the populace was illiterate and excluded from the political discourse.

    Local control of education also had its problems. These local school districts had different levels of wealth and so there was a difference in the quality of education provided. Slaves were often prohibited from receiving an education (although some did anyway) and after emancipation black schools were usually inferior to white schools. State governments and the federal government got involved to try and remedy these anomalies. Because government is charged with maintaining the social contract, this was an appropriate action to take. Although parents strive to give their children the best education, it is government's job to make sure that <u>all</u> children get a good education. This has brought parents and government into conflict over the education of children. Parents and government have different roles in society. Tension in society is not necessarily a bad thing and is inevitable in a diverse society as we have in America. Resistance training is necessary to build strong muscles and diverse opinions and views can strengthen society. A society without tension would be flaccid and flabby and would have difficulty resisting a stronger more vibrant culture or society.

    The high level of literacy was a key element powering America's rapid development in the nineteenth century. Other nations now also have high literacy rates so America has lost much of its educational competitive edge. Educational priorities in the United States have shifted away from educational rigor and the development of a democratic citizenry toward building self-esteem of students and the importance of communal values. Although we spend more per student than almost any other nation, our educational achievements are mediocre. Mediocre doesn't cut it.

Edifice of Trust

Diversity In Education

In order to have the best educational system we need to have diversity and competition among our educational choices. Competition and innovation are the driving forces of economic growth and the advancement of civilization. But education in America is failing to produce the educated citizenry that the nation will need on the 21st century. Progressives resist choice in education and strive to create a monolithic educational structure dominated by government and the teachers' unions. The goal of this monolith is to inculcate the communal values of progressivism in order to prepare students for life in the social welfare state. Achievement in learning is discouraged. Competition is athletics has been converted to participation trophies for everyone. Parents need alternatives to this attempted monopoly of education.

Luckily in America there are still educational options available.

Private/Boarding Schools

Private schools are the bastion of the elites where their children are not only provided a rigorous education but also form the relationships among their elite peers that will serve them in business and government for the rest of their lives. Even progressive presidents such as President Clinton and President Obama send their daughters to elite boarding schools in preparation for their future careers in politics.

Private schools highlight the difficulty of balancing our principles of personal freedom and equality of opportunity. Parents should have the freedom to select the best educational opportunities for their children. However it is in the national interest that all children have the best educational opportunities. In a free society we must tolerate some inequality because the ability to improve your circumstances (or those of your children) is a central driving force of human nature. Communalism, in its efforts to eliminate inequality, ends up destroying ambition by setting the bar to the lowest common denominator.

Charter Schools

Charter schools are an attempt to replicate the educational success of private schools for ordinary citizens. Charter schools can use innovative techniques that would be inappropriate at public schools (and greatly resisted by teachers' unions). Some have been very successful and some have not. But this is the nature of innovation and creative destruction. The unsuccessful ones disappear and the successful ones survive.

Many charter schools are targeted at minority communities because these communities have the fewest educational options. The problem for these minority communities is affordability. When their taxes (or the property taxes of their landlords) go solely to public schools, they have little money left to pay for charter schools. Some cities and states convert tax revenue into vouchers that parents can use at any school. Teachers' unions insist that tax monies should only go to public schools and vigorously oppose vouchers. But this is because they view the institution of public schools as more important than the education of the students.

Religious Schools

Religious schools can be a point of contention in a country where separation of church and state is the law of the land. But Catholic schools are well respected for their ability to provide quality education at a reasonable cost (because nuns are a lot cheaper than unionized teachers). Other religions can also provide quality education along with religious values (there is nothing wrong with religious values as long as it is not the state that is defining what those religious values are). And it is important that religious values don't interfere with getting an education equal to the highest standards so students graduating from religious schools must have been taught American civic values as well. But there is a potential conflict in teaching religious values with public funds. Many people (not just teachers' unions) oppose the use of taxes to support religious schools.

Home Schooling

Many parents prefer to home school their kids because they think that they can do a better job than the other educational options available. Home schooling however presents many challenges. Parents may lack the expert knowledge needed to teach certain subjects. And the kids do not have the opportunity to socialize with other kids and participate in extracurricular activities (although there are some home schooling associations that try and fill this gap). Still home schooling provides an educational option that should be available to parents.

Internet Schools

A new option that has recently become available is the development of Internet schools such as K12. These schools provide instruction over the Internet in real time and sometimes are under contract from the local school district. Internet instruction such as Khan Academy has proven beneficial as an educational supplement but the jury is still out on full time Internet learning. Nevertheless, schooling in the 21st century needs to be able to take advantage of technological innovations such as those offered by Khan Academy and K12.

Public Schools

Public schools have an honorable history in the United States. I went to a public school and got a pretty good preparation for college. Many other successful people went to America's public schools. In the past there wasn't so much need for educational alternatives because the public schools did a good job. But public schools have been coopted by a progressive agenda that has changed the focus of education away from excellence and toward mediocrity.

Edifice of Trust

Educational and athletic achievement are viewed negatively. The performance of winners is tainted by the hurt feelings of the losers. Public schools are not training the next leaders of America but the next entitlement recipients. This is why today's parents need educational options.

Remedial Schools

Even if we greatly improve the educational system, there will be students who have difficulty with the curriculum. This option would not be for students with disabilities that require a different kind of education. This would be for students who come from poor neighborhoods or broken homes or from substandard public schools that did not achieve the level of education needed to survive in the twenty-first century. Regional remedial schools may be necessary to help these students achieve the minimum levels of attainment. These schools could be public schools but could also be charter schools contracted by the school districts for these specialized programs.

Boot Camp

Even with the envisioned improvements in education contemplated in this book, there will be students that are not ready to join the work force or to apply for secondary education, especially in the period of transformation that will take years to achieve. Students may lack the study skills, language capabilities and social skills necessary to succeed in advanced education and in the work place. Businesses, local and national, know the skill sets needed for success in the workplace. Large national and multinational companies can afford to train unready workers but at great expense. Small business, however, usually cannot afford programs to prepare unready workers leaving them unable to find employment even at minimum wages. Curricula for the boot camps should be developed by the business community, which should also sponsor these programs because they will be the primary beneficiaries of a better educated workforce (in addition to the students). Colleges and universities would set up programs to teach students how to study and succeed at the secondary level. It would not be remedial education, but the life skills they need to succeed on a more independent level (even a well-educated kid can graduate from high school knowing trigonometry but not know how to balance a checkbook – maybe there's an app for that).

Competition and innovation are the key elements to the success of the free market economic system that has propelled the United States to be the richest, most powerful country in the world. There is no justifiable reason these principles should not be applied to education. The free market system creates winners and losers and some people think that this is not "fair". But in the Olympics only one person or one team wins the gold medal but all participants gain from the experience. We need an educational system that creates the winners that will be the future leaders of our country while assuring that all students gain from the educational experience. Not everybody can be a leader but we need an educated populace to assure the continuation of the Founders' vision.

Educational Standards

With all these different educational options, some form of national standards need to be established. There is a lot of dissatisfaction with the current standards testing but we need to develop methods for checking the student's readiness to move on to the next level as well as the schools performance in preparing its students. The teachers' unions resist these standards because they not only reflect the student's educational abilities but also the teacher's teaching ability. Educating our children is not an assembly line where teachers put little sprockets of knowledge into the heads of their students. So teachers are gifted and others are shlubs. Gifted teachers should be justly rewarded for their efforts (and we are not talking about Teacher of the Year awards unless they come with big fat bonus checks). Employers and secondary education institutions need to be able to rely on these tests and standards in making their decisions affecting the future of these students.

Edifice of Trust

<u>Secondary Education</u>
	The Clinton campaign came out for free college education and the elimination of 1.2 trillion dollars of student debts. As farfetched as this may seem there is a kernel of logic in such a proposal. In the nineteenth century farmers and most other workers only needed an elementary education to be prepared for life in America. Only a very small fraction of the people went on to higher education. In many areas of the United States this elementary education was funded by the local community as a public good. In the twentieth century factory workers and clerical staff needed a high school education to have the skills necessary for the industrialization of America. This high school education was usually paid for by the local community through property taxes. In the twenty-first century, a more advanced education is needed to have the skills required for the Internet Age. It would make sense to provide this advanced education if we could figure out a way to pay for it. The taxpayers need to benefit along with the students. Such a program would, like all government programs, be subject to waste, abuse and outright fraud. I would make the program as simple and transparent as possible, a stipend to students in good standing at qualified institutions. The stipend would be the same for all students whether they went to Harvard or community college. The stipend would be for four years only. It could be extended only if the student was a graduate student in good standing at a qualified university.
	The cost will be enormous so the benefit must be even larger. Contented, debt-free students is not a sufficient benefit. Such largesse can be justified only if it benefits the entire nation by making its population better educated and more productive. We would not be doing this out of the goodness of our hearts or because we are nice people with good motives (the progressive's standard). We need to get results or cut the program. Students receiving the stipend should become productive workers not taxicab drivers (a job reserved for Pakistani immigrants until they can learn English). The government is already covering a large part of advanced education through its student loan guarantee program because it has to cover the huge amount of defaulted student loans. The government needs to get out of the business of

guaranteeing loans where it has no control of the risk factors (amount of loan and ability to repay). For-profit colleges would have to change their business strategies of loading up students with huge debts when the colleges are put on the hook for defaults.

The stipend would be modest and students and universities would be expected to contribute to covering the costs. This stipend is intended for education not football programs.

If the average worker began his career in the nineteenth century at age 15-16, and the twentieth century worker at the age of 18-19, the twenty-first century worker will begin his or her career at the age of 22-23. The later development of worker skills combined with longer life imply that the work career should be extended from current levels. We need to rethink retirement ages in light of these changing demographics .

Edifice of Trust

Student Rights

  The educational process must be designed to prepare students to become citizens. Kindergartners lack the maturity and education to be full participants in the social contract. They are dependent on their parents and teachers to guide them in the right direction, to teach them proper behavior and give them the knowledge they need to live in a modern society. These little kids do not have rights so much as protections. They need to be protected from adult society and they need to be protected from themselves. They lack the education and maturity to make good decisions. Therefore, they cannot yet be allowed to freely exercise their rights in society.

  As students advance through grade school, junior high school and high school, they gain in knowledge and maturity. They earn more rights to make their own decisions. Some of these decisions are not wise but that is part of the learning process. The important thing is to make sure that these unwise decisions do not cause permanent damage to themselves or others. They need to learn how to live within the framework of society. They need to know the rules and regulations, the extent of their rights within the framework and their obligations to other people that live and work within the framework. As little children this framework is very restrictive and as they grow and mature the framework expands and gives them greater personal freedom. But children are too self-centered to understand their obligations and responsibilities within society.

Edifice of Trust

Giving students too many rights but an incomplete understanding of their responsibilities results in the chaotic mess that afflicts many of our public schools. This is the result of a progressive philosophy that transforms rights into entitlements and ignores a citizen's responsibilities. Progressives do not expect people to be responsible. That (they think) is the role of government. A progressive education is an education in victimhood. It teaches that elites have unjustifiably taken all the wealth and that people need the coercive power of government to wrest this wealth from the "one-percenters" in order for them to receive their entitlements. It doesn't teach responsibility but political correctness. They need safe zones to protect them from "hate speech" so that they can continually wallow in their victimhood.

These are not the principles that America was founded on. And this is not an education that prepares student to take on the responsibilities of citizenship in a democratic society. It is a preparation for communalism and socialism. A principled policy will give students the freedoms they earn as they learn and mature. The schools are microcosms of the greater society and if the schools are chaotic and disorderly we are looking at our future.

Edifice of Trust

Principled Policy Options In Education

Public education as currently being provided is failing to serve the nation and its citizens. It is not preparing students for a successful life in the twenty-first century but only to be recipients of social welfare programs. In order for public education policy to better serve the nation we need to base educational policies on the American Founding Principles. Students need to be prepared to know their rights and responsibilities as future citizens of the social contract. They need to know the history of the United States and why, despite its flaws and failures, it is the greatest nation on Earth. They need to understand the philosophical basis for our western values and why American exceptionalism can help the entire world. Because public education is failing in this responsibility, we need to provide parents and students with options that will achieve these goals. Giving a monopoly on education to progressive socialists to push their communalist agenda will spell the end of America and douse the light it provides to the world.

In order to adequately prepare our youth to lead America into the future, we need:

1. School choice. Parents need options for the education of their children. Competition has helped create the economic success of the United States and it can do the same for education.

2. Vouchers. Just as we are advocating the portability of health insurance, the tax support of education should follow the kids wherever they go to school.

3. Year-round school. American school children do not need the entire summer off to help tend the family farm. More and more two-income families or single parent families mean parents do not have the time flexibility to adjust their work to school schedules. School schedules need to reflect the economic realities of today's parents.

4. College stipend. The potential cost of this program requires further study. We need to make sure that the nation will benefit from this additional expense. One method of reducing the cost of the program would be to eliminate government guaranteed student loans. The stipend should also be available for certain kinds of vocational training.

5. Educational Standards. School choice requires uniform standards to assure that all the different types of education are achieving the goal of having better educated kids. The standards can be used to find bright kids that can advance more quickly as well as identify those kids that need additional help.

Edifice of Trust

Chapter 8

Is Healthcare A Civil Right?

The Right to Healthcare?

Do people have a right to public provided healthcare? Many People in Europe believe in public healthcare. France and the United Kingdom have single-payer systems funded by the taxpayers. People over there like government provided healthcare. But then they are comfortable with very large government providing a lot of services in addition to healthcare.

Progressives would like to install a single-payer healthcare system in the United States. They would also like the government to provide many more services as is common in much of Europe. Is that so wrong? Could the progressives (and the Europeans) be right?

I would say yes, of course. Of course as long as there was a country or power that could keep us safe, that would be a beacon of freedom to the world, that would be the defender of western civilization. Europe relies on America for this role. It was America that supplied the financial resources to help Europe recover from two devastating world wars. It was America that held the Red Army at bay and kept most of Europe out of the grip of the Soviets. It was America that gave Europe a seat at the table in the post war institutions that

Edifice of Trust

were the framework of a world order that has prevented major wars for seventy years. And it was America that opened its markets to European manufacturers to enable them to rebuild their economies and employment.

Wait a minute you might be saying. I am conflating two different things; healthcare and America's role in the world. But I don't think I am. America is different. America is a country that was established based on the philosophy of John Locke and other Enlightenment philosophers that said legal authority is derived from the people, not from government. The people are sovereign.

European countries have existed for many centuries under many different forms of government. Monarchies and dictatorships wax and wane but these countries continue. That is the case of most countries. But America is different. America was founded based on ideas and principles. America is bound by these principles. Change these principles and America will cease to exist. There will be a country. It might be called America. But it won't be America.

What does all this have to do with healthcare?

Everything! The American people have employed personal and economic liberty to create the richest, most powerful country on earth. It doesn't matter that our TVs are made in China, Japan and Korea. It was the power of competition that drove the price of TVs down while the quality improved with each passing year. Innovation and competition are the driving forces of the free market economic system that is upheld by the post-war institutions created by the United States and its allies.

The forces of competition and innovation exist in the healthcare industry as well but government meddling has distorted these forces to create a system that is inefficient and very expensive. The US spends about 17% of GDP on healthcare compared to about 11% in France and 9% in the UK. Healthcare expenses are necessary but not directly productive. Think about it. Unless you are a doctor, you spend money on healthcare so that you have a happy, productive life. But if too much of your time and money is devoted to your healthcare, you have less time and money for more productive uses. It is the same on a national basis. The six to eight percentage points' difference means that France and the UK have that money to spend on other things.

Edifice of Trust

Both the French and British healthcare systems were created soon after the Second World War. These systems were created in their entirety and the structures have changed relatively little since. After the war, the United States, having escaped the devastation inflicted on Europe, had an intact private healthcare system. The Federal government, while perhaps well intentioned, got into healthcare in dribs and drabs. First by providing a tax benefit to employers who provided health insurance for their employees. This benefit allowed employers to deduct the cost of the healthcare benefits provided to employees while the employees were not required to pay taxes on the benefits they received lieu of salary. So employees got a raise but the company did not have to pay any more than it was already.

But dribs and drabs, and partial reforms and improvements usually don't provide the anticipated benefits. There are side effects and unintended consequences. Originally, health insurance was intended to pay for only unexpected expenses or major procedures. Routine expenses like doctor visits and medicines were paid for out-of-pocket. But out-of-pocket money is after tax money. If those routine expenses were routed through the employer's insurance company they would be tax-free. So slowly more and more procedures and costs were routed through the employer's insurance company. Eventually, the insurance ceased to be insurance and became just a giant tax-exempt payment system (a very inefficient and costly one).

In order to save taxes, employees paid less and less of their healthcare costs directly. It has got to the point that some people gripe about having to pay a token co-pay of $10. No one wants to pay any of his or her healthcare costs anymore. They want it to be free. It is their right!

But it isn't really free. Somebody has to pay the healthcare costs and US costs are more than almost any other country. People just want somebody else to pay for it.

But prior to the Obama administration not everybody worked for an employer that provided healthcare coverage. Further, some people were independent contractors or self-employed. Some only worked part-time or were unemployed. These people had to come up with their own payment system.

Edifice of Trust

They bought their own health insurance with their after-tax dollars or they went without coverage. Many of those without coverage were poor. The poor would wait until their condition got so bad that they would have to go to the emergency room. There they would receive emergency care the cost of which was usually borne by the hospital. Not a very efficient mechanism for healthcare delivery.

The whole system was in need of reform. However, the Affordable Care Act (better known as Obamacare) was not the answer. It was the rush to approve Obamacare that generated the famous quote by then Speaker of the House Nancy Pelosi, "we have to pass the bill so that you can find out what is in it". A bill deliberately made complex in order to generate confusion (according to Jonathan Gruber who helped the Obama administration draft the Affordable Care Act). The law changed employer health insurance from a benefit provided voluntarily by employers to a legal requirement enforced by the IRS. The law requires the healthy to get insurance so there will be funds to pay for the sick. The bill requires men to pay for insurance that provides coverage for birth control medicine. The bill requires everyone to get insurance or to join a healthcare exchange or be subject to a fine. But only sick people have joined the exchanges (the healthy preferred to pay a fine). As a result the insurance companies participating in the exchanges have lost billions. Many are stopping the hemorrhage by leaving the exchanges and the entire system looks likely to collapse.

Progressives insist the answer is even more government involvement. Many feel that the collapse of Obamacare will morph into a single payer system like many European countries. Some cynics might even suggest that was the actual goal of Obamacare.

But is healthcare really an inalienable right in the same sense as life, liberty and the pursuit of happiness? The Constitution makes no mention of it. Other human needs such as food and shelter are more urgent. But there is no "right" to food and shelter. We have to pay for that out of our pocket. Only the poorest of us in the US lack for food and shelter. It is true that the poor receive assistance in the form of food stamps, public housing, etc. But is that a right or

Edifice of Trust

charity? Is it a stopgap, or a way of life? Once they have sufficient money they are expected to pay for these needs themselves.

Not so healthcare. Everyone expects healthcare to be provided for them. Why is that? If left to their own free will many people would divert money from healthcare to other (sometimes even frivolous) expenses. They would even divert money toward purchases such as alcohol or tobacco that will make their health worse. Even the healthy are guilty because they do not purchase health insurance when they don't need it (or they only get a catastrophic policy with a very high deductible). They don't contribute to the insurance pool so the sick are stuck in a pool with other sick people.

So the only way to cover the sick people is to force everyone, including the healthy, to join in the insurance pool. So what happened to our personal liberty? In order to get the money for sick people you and I lose the right to make the decisions about our own health. Is the right to make our own decisions about healthcare one of the non-essential liberties that Benjamin Franklin was talking about? Do we need to cede this liberty so that the social contract can function better?

It wasn't one of the rights the Founders considered or it would have been in the Constitution. But times have changed. Doctors back then were quacks (or dentists), medicine was snake oil and hospitals were places people went to die (well that part hasn't changed). In this modern era, I might be willing to cede my right to make my own decisions about healthcare if I were convinced (as progressives are) that this was not just for the public good, but the only way to achieve this public good. I am not willing to make that concession yet because I don't think we have investigated alternatives that are in accordance with our American principles. We have been led into a swamp by our guides who insist they are the only ones that can save us by leading deeper into the swamp.

During the 2016 election, progressives told us that we have no alternative but to save Obamacare or millions of people will be without healthcare and tens of thousands will die as a result. But we can't just go back to

Edifice of Trust

the status quo ante. We are stuck in a swamp and we have to pick our way out. Slowly. Carefully.

There are a number of reforms that we can begin to implement now but we have to remember that the current system has been in development for over fifty years and it will be difficult to untangle the mess. We have tremendous legacy problems. I have been contributing to Medicare ever since it was created in 1966. I need to receive a benefit from all those funds I contributed, as do all the other folks that did so as well. And I plan to live a good long time so Medicare will be paying and paying. The Congressional Budget Office estimates the unfunded liability of Medicare is up to $36.9 trillion although I have heard higher estimates than that.

Edifice of Trust

The Fate Of Obamacare

The Clinton campaign boldly asserted that people have a right to affordable healthcare but she took the concept of a right and twisted it into an unrecognizable shape. Our Enlightenment philosophers and our Founders stated that the people have natural rights and that the people cede certain rights to the government to form the social contract. Rights not ceded are retained by the people (or the states). A right, then, is freedom from government. Under Mrs. Clinton's conception, a right becomes a service provided by government, making the people not free from government but dependent on government. Her campaign promised universal healthcare for everyone in America. Because Obamacare would have failed no matter who was elected president, some new plan had to be created to replace Obamacare. If Mrs. Clinton had been elected, we would have been well down the road toward a European-style single payer system.

However, Mrs. Clinton lost, at least in part because of her support for Obamacare. On the campaign trail, now-President Trump promised to eliminate Obamacare on day one. Well into his administration, however, Obamacare is still continuing its slow-motion breakdown dance. Joe Kernan was right when he said on his morning show on CNBC, Squawk Box, that the Democrats had pulled one over on the Republicans because you can never take back an entitlement. If even one poor bloke is featured on the MSM (Main Stream Media) moaning that he is dying because he lost his healthcare coverage because of the Republicans they are toast in the next election.

Edifice of Trust

Actually, I am not surprised that Obamacare is still twisting in the wind as of this writing. Our healthcare fiasco is many decades in the making and cannot be undone overnight. The Republicans under the leadership of House Speaker Paul Ryan have come up with a plan that would repeal Obamacare and replace it with a new plan. But as Joe Kernan noted, you can't take back entitlements. The Ryan plan keeps a lot of Obamacare goodies. Conservatives in the Congress call it Obamacare-lite. Much of his program is an amalgam of tax credits, tax exemptions and other tax gymnastics to cajole people into doing the right things (marginally better than using force as the Democrats prefer but not by much). Republicans use taxes much like Democrats use spending, and to much the same effect. Tax subsidies hide the true cost of programs and use tax incentives to manipulate people. The principled argument is they should leave out all the tax subsidies and incentives and just use taxes to fund the government. That way citizens can better understand how the government operates and see what their taxes are used for (for a more detailed analysis of taxes and tax reform please see my earlier book, *Principled Policy*, or my pamphlet *The Principles of Taxation*.

Here are some principled-based policies that would make sense.

End double tax exemption

During the campaign, President Trump said he wanted to expand the double exemption to include the self-employed and independent contractors. But it is the double exemption that started us on the messed up path we are currently on. We need to end the double tax exemption that has distorted the pricing mechanism of the free market economic system along with all the other tax incentives and subsidies that distort the market. If the government wants to provide healthcare benefits then it should go to Congress to approve a disbursement to that effect. In this way we will have a very clear picture of how our tax monies are being spent.

Edifice of Trust

End employer insurance plans
What began as a perquisite to attract top talent has become an onerous burden. But it is not just a burden for the employer but also the employee. Many people are afraid to leave their current employer because they might lose their medical insurance. We need to divorce the healthcare system from employers so that the people will have freedom in making their healthcare decisions independent of their employment decisions. Employer based healthcare is an anachronism of the 1950's. 21st century employment is very different.

Make insurance portable
Medical policies should be with individuals or families, not companies. This way people will not lose their insurance when they change jobs. If the company wants to pick up all or part of the tab as a voluntary benefit, that's fine (but people will pay tax on the benefit as it is additional income). People change jobs and careers over their lifetime and we need a healthcare system that keeps that in mind.

Make a market in pre-existing conditions
One of the principal failures of the old healthcare system was the treatment of pre-existing conditions. Once a person was diagnosed with a serious chronic condition he or she was virtually trapped in their current insurance policy (and employment) because no other insurance company would provide insurance or would charge enormous fees to cover the cost of treatment. We need a market for pre-existing conditions. A company insuring a chronic condition would be happy to pay another company to take the policy off their hands if they thought their upfront costs would be less than the net present value of covering the future medical costs. Another company might be willing to accept the policy if they felt the upfront payment they would receive would offset the future cost of coverage. This market place mechanism would allow patients greater flexibility in getting the proper coverage for their condition. Why would insurers enter into a transaction like this? For the same

reason bond traders buy and sell US Treasury bonds. They have different viewpoints on the direction of interest rates so they are constantly buying and selling bonds. Likewise, an insurance company may believe that medical advances will reduce the future cost of coverage and so will be willing to take on a policy from an insurer that has a different viewpoint.

Allow the importation of prescription drugs

The development cost of new drugs is enormous but the marginal production costs are miniscule. Pharmaceutical companies in the United States get all their profit from new drugs while other countries (the single payer systems) can negotiate better deals for US drugs because they are buying in bulk for an entire country. Allowing the importation of these drugs back from other countries would reduce costs for patients in the US. The ban on re-importation gives the pharmaceutical companies monopoly pricing power in the US. Further, Congress has barred Medicare from negotiating drug prices to lower costs. Creating a liquid market for these drugs (assuming there are controls to prevent counterfeits) would increase competition and lower prices. (in the world of finance this is called arbitrage and it is one of the mechanisms that allows prices to adjust in the free market system).

Ratings for doctors and hospitals

As we get back to making more of our own decisions about our healthcare we will need more information on how to evaluate alternatives. Doctors' associations hide relevant information like the track record of doctors and how often they are sued for malpractice. It is also difficult to get statistics on how many people die from infections at particular hospitals. While medical decisions are complicated, technology can go a long way to give us the information we need to make appropriate decisions.

Make people pay for a larger portion of their medical bills.

There is no free lunch. Medical costs are high and going higher because our messed up system has destroyed the pricing mechanism. We need to

Edifice of Trust

release the power of the free market to work in the healthcare sector. While most covered medical procedures have increased in cost, Lasik surgery (not covered) has gone down in cost as the surgeries have become safer and more effective with new and improved techniques driven by free market incentives.

Many people might think these reforms are radical and that they will greatly increase their cost of healthcare. But the goal is to reduce the cost of healthcare and make it more efficient. The free market economic system has done this for other products and other industries for years. It can do it for healthcare as well. There may have to be a lengthy transition period. It has taken 60 years to arrive at our current messed up situation and it will take some time to undo the damage.

The need to reform healthcare encompasses more than just better serving the needs of the people. We also need to do it for our country. Currently we spend about 17% of GDP on healthcare. The rest of the developed world spends around 10%. Worse yet, as our population ages, healthcare is destined increase as a percentage of our GDP. If the progressives get their way healthcare expenses will explode. But healthcare is not a very productive way to spend our money.

Let's take a look at a business, let's say a manufacturing company. The company's goal is to produce a product to sell and make a profit. Company management realizes that they need to spend a certain amount of their revenues to keep their factories operating at peak efficiency. But any money spent on maintenance is money that is not available for R&D to develop new products, to pay for labor to expand production, etc. So the maintenance budget must be kept in balance to assure future profitability and competitiveness.

Excessive healthcare expenses are sapping the strength of our nation and making us less competitive in a world that is becoming more competitive and dangerous. Progressives would take us further down the path of diverting precious resources to healthcare and other social welfare programs, dedicating more and more of our economy to healthcare and other government-provided services while eviscerating our economic power and defunding our defenses.

Edifice of Trust

These principled reforms will reintroduce healthcare to the free market system and will result in lower costs and greater efficiency. This will not only benefit the individual citizen but also the national economy.

Government intervention in the healthcare market, while perhaps well-intentioned, has had the net result of creating an unholy healthcare mess. Day one solutions, as promised by Candidate Trump, make for good campaign promises but are impractical and unwise in reality. The structure of the entire healthcare system has been distorted by government programs, subsidies and mandates. President Trump and Paul Ryan double down further involving government in our personal healthcare. The extrication of government from the healthcare system will be a long and complex process. Many citizens are deeply investing in the current system and sudden changes could have a devastating impact on their health and finances.

Efforts to insulate people from healthcare costs have resulted in the incessant upward spiral of healthcare costs to the extent they are crowding out other necessary expenditures on a national basis. Any reform of healthcare and medical insurance will require patients to bear some of the costs so that the free market pricing mechanism can work to increase competition and efficiency.

Edifice of Trust

Chapter 9

Gun Violence

America's Gun Violence Epidemic

Gun violence and gun control laws are perennial targets of the Democrats and other progressives. America seems to beset by horrific mass murders recently such as the massacre in Orlando Florida that killed 49. Chicago is a sea of blood with 455 murders as of August 2016 compared to 490 in all of 2015 (over 90% were shot and over 70% were black). Mrs. Clinton railed against gun violence and vowed in her campaign platform to increase gun control. Progressive media and policy institutes publish lurid diatribes against the American Gun Violence Epidemic.

My trusty dictionary (New World Dictionary of the English Language) defines epidemic (from the Greek epi – among and demos – the people) as something prevalent and spreading rapidly among many individuals in a community. Let's take a look at what is actually going on.

It is true that the United States has the most guns per capita of any country in the world with a total of 88.8 guns per hundred according to the Small Arms Survey published by the Geneva Graduate Institute. Our progressive friends assert that because of all those guns the US has the highest murder rate per capita of all the developed nations. It is true that the US ranks 108th out of 218 nations in the number of deaths per capita as rated by the United Nations Office of Drugs and Crime (UNODC). And it is true that about two-thirds of murders in the US are by guns. And our progressive friends would have you believe that as the number of guns in America increases so do the number of deaths by gun violence.

But let's look at the facts. The UNODC study also notes that Europe (relatively small homogenous countries compared to the US) and Asia have low murder rates (3.0 and 2.9 per 100,000, respectively) compared to the world average of 6.2. The US rate Of 3.9 per 100,000 is somewhat above the European average but well below the average of Africa (12.5) and Latin America (16.3). Keep in mind that about 30% of the US population comes from Latin America and Africa. The black murder rate is eight times that of whites while the Hispanic murder is twice that of whites.

There is one more fact we need to take into account before we start drawing conclusions. The Swiss (peaceful little Switzerland) have the third most guns per capita in the world at 45.7 per 100 of population. Yet the murder rate in Switzerland is only 0.5 per 100,000 according to the UNODC, ranking as one of the least violent countries at 12th among the 218 countries in the study.

Gee, I guess it looks like guns don't kill people. People kill people. Less simplistically, the root causes of gun violence and murder in the United States are more complex than progressives would have you believe and less susceptible to the remedies they are trying to push on us. Might there be a reason for this? Let us continue our analysis.

Epidemic? What Epidemic?

The Clinton campaign and the Democratic platform boldly announced that there was an epidemic of gun violence in America. This point is buttressed regularly by the liberal media and think tanks. Mrs. Clinton lost the 2016 election but attacks on Second Amendment rights will be prominently featured in future campaigns. But what are the facts about this epidemic?

Edifice of Trust

Murder rates in America have declined and have been declining since 1991. Substantially so. The overall murder rate is down 42% and the absolute number is down 31%. These figures from the census bureau don't break out the murder by type of weapon but guns generally account for around two-thirds of all murders. So murder by firearms has likely also declined. The murder rate for black men has also declined substantially, around 45%, so their number of murders by gun violence has also declined.

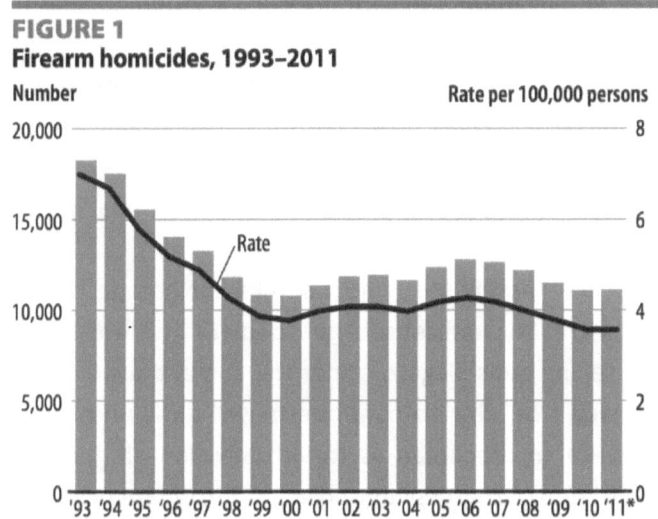

FIGURE 1
Firearm homicides, 1993–2011

Note: Excludes homicides due to legal intervention and operations of war. See appendix table 1 for numbers and rates.
*Preliminary estimates retrieved from Hoyert DL, Xu JQ. (2012) Deaths: Preliminary data for 2011. *National Vital Statistics Reports*, 61(6).
Source: Centers for Disease Control and Prevention, National Center for Injury Prevention and Control. Web-based Injury Statistics Query and Reporting System (WISQARS), 1993–2010. Retrieved March 2013 from www.cdc.gov/ncipc/wisqars.

The website for the Clinton campaign highlighted in big red numbers the figure of 33,636 as the number of people who have died as a result of gun violence. What they don't tell you is that most of those deaths were suicides. About half of all suicides were by firearms. And it is true that the suicide rate has increased from 10.9 per 100,000 in 2005 to 12.9 in 2014, an increase of 18%. But the suicide rate per100,000 from 1950 through 1970 was around 13 so suicide is an endemic problem, not an epidemic problem.

Edifice of Trust

The Clinton campaign proposed a number of gun control measures but these measures were unlikely to have had much affect on the "epidemic of gun violence". One of her promises was to close the "gun show loophole" where individuals can sell guns without a background check. The Clinton campaign said this happens "frequently" but a review by Politifact found that most guns sales at gun shows were by licensed dealers who did background checks and would not be impacted by closing the loophole.

Closing the loophole would impact me (or you) if I wanted to sell my gun at a gun show because none of my family or friends wanted to buy it (which is legal). I would have to get a license to sell the gun and would be required to do a background check (which I have no idea how to do). The proposal to cut-off the "gun show loophole" and other gun control measures will have their greatest impact on legal gun owners like me while having only a minimal impact on reducing gun violence.

It is true that there are "hobbyists" who do take advantage of this loophole because they are, in reality, unlicensed gun dealers and are selling guns illegally. But if they are selling guns illegally under the current law it would be naïve to think that they won't be able to continue to sell guns under new laws (unless the new laws were so draconian as to virtually ban all gun sells entirely which would be fine to most progressives and gun control fanatics).

People perpetrating violent crimes with guns rarely do so with legal guns. The numbers are fuzzy because the guns related to these crimes are often not recovered making it impossible to check their legality. In a survey in Cook County jail only 2 felons out of 70 that had guns had purchased their guns legally. A study by the Department of Justice showed that only 7.3% of prison inmates purchased their gun from a retail store and less than one percent from gun shows.

TABLE 14
Source of firearms possessed by state prison inmates at time of offense, 1997 and 2004

	Percent of state prison inmates	
Source of firearm	1997	2004
Total	100%	100%
Purchased or traded from—	14.0%	11.3%
Retail store	8.2	7.3
Pawnshop	4.0	2.6
Flea market	1.0	0.6
Gun show	0.8	0.8
Family or friend	40.1%	37.4%
Purchased or traded	12.6	12.2
Rented or borrowed	18.9	14.1
Other	8.5	11.1
Street/illegal source	37.3%	40.0%
Theft or burglary	9.1	7.5
Drug dealer/off street	20.3	25.2
Fence/black market	8.0	7.4
Other	8.7%	11.2%

Note: Includes only inmates with a current conviction. Estimates may differ from previously published BJS reports. To account for differences in the 1997 and 2004 inmate survey questionnaires, the analytical methodology used in 1997 was revised to ensure comparability with the 2004 survey.

Source: Bureau of Justice Statistics, Survey of Inmates in State and Federal Correctional Facilities, 1997 and 2004.

Where there has been an epidemic it has been in the media coverage of mass murder events that has stoked the public reaction. Within minutes of these tragic events (and often while the event is still in progress) the remote video trucks of the local (and quickly the national) news outlets arrive on the scene to begin their non-stop broadcasting. The unfolding of these events proceeds slowly so most of the coverage is repetition of what was already known and interviews of so-called experts who speculate on the event with little or no knowledge of the facts. All this coverage generates hysteria and calls for more gun control so that such an event "can never happen again".

After each such event, gun sales spike. But they do not spike because the public fears such violence, they spike because the public fears their right to bear arms will be infringed (another way of saying taken away).

Edifice of Trust

New gun control laws are unlikely to have a major impact on violent gun crimes. They are also unlikely to affect the suicide rate that has held fairly steady over seven decades very much. This is just another example of the progressive "what works" philosophy. If they don't like the numbers, they try and force the numbers to change without addressing the underlying causes of the numbers. In the case of gun deaths we are talking poverty and mental health.

The War on Drugs

The War on Drugs, announced by President Nixon in 1971, has been a contributing factor in the number of homicides through gun violence. The War on Drugs impacts the nation in three ways; the gun violence and other related crimes perpetrated by drug gangs in the United States, the gun violence and other related crimes perpetrated by drug gangs in Central and South America which dwarfs the number recorded in the United States, and the flow of people trying to escape drug related violence in Central and South America by fleeing to the United States.

Even though gang members account for less than one-half of one percent of the US population (numbers are estimates), gang violence accounted for about 10 percent of all gun related homicides according to the FBI. In Mexico, the drug wars are estimated to have left over 111,000 dead while in Honduras and El Salvador the murder rate is 84.6 and 64.2, respectively. Millions of people have fled this violence and crossed illegally into the United States. In recent years the numbers of unaccompanied minors has swelled because these kids are the ones that are forcefully recruited into the gangs.

The murder rate in the United States (as well as Mexico and Central America) will continue to outpace other regions of the world so long as we continue this futile war. The Hollywood types that gather to sing songs of protest against gun violence are the same ones that go backstage and snort cocaine.

Edifice of Trust

<u>The Reason We Have the Second Amendment</u>
When talking about gun control it is important to remember what happened in Tiananmen Square on June 4, 1989. I know that was over 25 years ago and that is just forever for many of you folks (because history is boring). But there is an important lesson to be learned.

Many people in China felt that the opening up of the country since the death of Mao Zedong in 1976 would lead eventually to more freedom and possibly democracy. In the spring of 1989, Chinese college students and other young people began to demonstrate around the country and to stage sit-ins to peacefully push for greater democracy. These protests were across the country but the main focus was in Tiananmen Square, which is just in front of the Forbidden City (the Chinese Imperial Palace for over 500 years). The Chinese communist government had no intention of loosening its grip on the country. On the night of June 3rd, government troops and tanks moved to clear out the protestors killing hundreds (possibly thousands – the Chinese government figures are considered unreliable by many people). It was a massacre. The Chinese protesters had no weapons with which to defend themselves.

This brutal act of the Chinese communist government is a prime example of the use of the coercive power of the state so feared by our Founding Fathers. They felt that a central government with a powerful standing army was an inherent threat to any democracy; especially one so fragile and new as America's in 1789. The Founders wrote the Second Amendment to address two issues related to the national militia. As a frontier country, the individual states maintained militias to provide protection from the dangers of the frontier and to support the standing army in case of invasion by foreign powers. But the second reason, as stated by Founding Father James Madison in his Federalist Paper #46, was that the Founders feared the coercive power of the central government and its standing army and felt that the armed militia would be a counterbalance to this power.

This is the reason the constitutional protection to keep and bear arms is so strong. Further, the Founders weren't protecting squirrel guns. In order to counterbalance the power of the central government's standing army, they were protecting the right to keep and bear military grade weapons (Swiss men keep their service weapons in their homes to this day).

But are the Founders' fears still relevant today or is the Second Amendment an anachronism of the eighteenth century? Even a powerful weapon like the AR-15 is useless against an Abrams tank or an F-35. And while the coercive power of the central government grows inexorably every day, it is the government bureaucrats and not the standing army where the power grows. The citizens demand this ever-increasing growth every time they vote for an expansion of the benefits and entitlements of the welfare state or plead that the government "do something" to reduce unemployment (getting out of the way of the private sector being insufficiently proactive).

So how are we to protect our precious freedoms against this encroaching tide of centralized power? Here again we can take a lesson from China. Just because the Square of Tiananmen is clear except for tourists and soldiers of the Peoples' Army doesn't mean there are no Chinese freedom fighters. Booksellers in Hong Kong have been publishing books considered subversive by the government in Beijing. These booksellers have been kidnapped and transported to Mainland China for incarceration and interrogation. No trials. No lawyers. After many months, and after a forced confession of their sins, they reappear chastened.

The Chinese communist leaders fear (and justifiably so) the ability of the people to communicate among themselves and to speak freely. They censor the Internet. They push domestic smartphones that have backdoors to government surveillance (and the biggest pirate of intellectual property in the world blocks the sale of iPhones on the basis of patent infringement). They arrest artists and intellectuals that don't toe the line. It wasn't guns that overthrew repressive regimes in the color revolutions (the Orange Revolution in Ukraine and the Rose Revolution in Georgia, for example). The spontaneous eruptions of the Arab Spring weren't back up with firepower. It was the will of the people and their ability to communicate that drove those revolutions.

But there are attacks on our ability to communicate here in America as well. Academia is well known for suppressing speech and thought that does not

Edifice of Trust

meet the far-left litmus test. The FBI is pushing Apple to create backdoors for their devices just like China. Rhode Island Senator Sheldon Whitehouse (D-RI) wants to use the organized crime RICO law against climate-change deniers. And just now in response to the Orlando massacre by an Afghan-American Muslim, the Department of Justice expunged all reference to Islam and ISIS from its release of the transcripts of the police tapes of the incident.

Our freedoms are being eroded bit by bit but your guns are useless in this fight. The weapons of modern governments are more subtle and insidious: manipulation of the media and control over the means of communication, creeping habituation to transfer payments and entitlements, regulations and mandates for private industry. Why would a modern government need to resort to guns? Egypt's guns could not stop the Arab Spring but the Egyptian Army was able to take over the subsequent democratically elected government without firing a shot.

The assault on the second amendment is only one flank of a full-fledged campaign to subject our individual liberty and freedom to the will of the collective. They try to convert our voluntary associations into government agencies. They define expressing an opinion in opposition to their programs as "hate speech". They are willing to violate the constitution (including the Second Amendment) to achieve their goals. These inroads on our freedom must be resisted. The best weapon in our arsenal is our ability to speak freely and to communicate with our fellow citizens. This must be protested at all costs.

Edifice of Trust

Principled Policies to Reduce Gun Violence

The Trump campaign website actually had a fairly good set of recommendations to further reduce gun violence in America. Hopefully these policies will be implemented now that Mr. Trump is president.

1. <u>Enforce existing laws.</u> This just makes sense. If some retail transactions are not subjected to background checks it is because of faults in the system and not the law. The database needs to be upgraded, coordinated and no-fly lists included. "Hobbyists" who are, in fact, unlicensed dealers need to be subject to all the existing laws. By enforcing existing laws we can greatly eliminate "loopholes" without infringing on the rights of law-abiding citizens.

2. <u>Reform mental health.</u> In the 60's and 70's mentally ill people were taken out of mental institutions and dumped on the street. This was partly due to humanitarian reasons (the mental institutions were horrid cesspools), good intentions (even the mentally ill have rights) and budget constraints (isn't it wonderful when good intentions and humanitarian instincts can reduce the budget deficit. What a wonderful world!). However these people had been institutionalized for a reason and out on their own and without treatment they just got worse. Proper mental health treatment plus institutionalization when necessary would help greatly in reducing violence and suicide. Dumping the mentally (whether in institutions or on the streets) is not part of the Social Contract.

Edifice of Trust

3. <u>Reduce poverty.</u> Poverty reduction was not mentioned by Mr. Trump but obviously if we are going to attack the root causes of crime and violence we need to attack poverty. We have been attacking poverty since the Johnson administration and the War on Poverty has been as woefully unsuccessful as the War on Drugs. The welfare system may have reduced the need of poor people but it also took their hope of betterment. It is hope that will help them rise out of poverty. A person with hope will refrain from violence so as to not jeopardize their future. A person with no hope has no future to jeopardize, so what the hell.

4. <u>End the War on Drugs</u>. About half the people in federal prisons are there for drug violations. A large percentage of gun violence is related to gang activity. Changing how we approach drug addiction will not only ease gun violence in the US it will break the back of violence in Central and South America (a number of Latin ex-presidents have come out in favor of legalization) and ease immigration pressures.

Edifice of Trust

Chapter 10

Terror

The Destruction of Trust

The goal of terrorists is to destroy the trust between citizens that is an essential part of the social contract. The edifice of trust is the framework for the social contract that binds citizens together. They want to break down that edifice of trust. They want us to turn on each other. They want us to be so consumed by fear that we begin to violate our sacred principles to try and protect ourselves. So although terrorism is typically a national security issue, the goal of terrorism is to destroy our social fabric, weaken our institutions and let us destroy ourselves from within.

We are already in the thrall of the terrorists. Every time we board an airplane we have to take off our shoes (because of one lame terrorist fool), belts, and jackets. We have to buy tiny bottles of shampoo and toothpaste (that cost as much as full size). They are already winning the war by making us run around airports in our sock feet. I doubt they even try to blow up planes in America any more. They already have us dancing to their tune. Time to find another weak spot to attack.

Edifice of Trust

Terrorists are smart. They will attack any soft target where people gather; sports venues, market places, airports and railroad stations. They will use unconventional weapons such as box cutters, fertilizer, 18-wheelers and delivery vans. The attackers will be hard-core jihadists or women and children under duress. They are trying to make us distrust everyone and everything.

The standard reaction of politicians to a terror event is to propose some policy so that such a terroristic event will "never happen again". You must realize that this is an impossible statement to make. Of course it will happen again. But politicians hate to be seen as weak or ineffectual. They have to do something (more importantly they have to be <u>seen</u> doing something). But not every action to defend the lives of innocent civilians can be justified. Only principled action can be justified. Unprincipled action betrays our founding principles and make us little better that the terrorists.

The words of Benjamin Franklin are particularly relevant here. Let me repeat: "They who can give up essential liberty to obtain a little temporary safety deserve neither liberty nor safety".

Remember, a central thesis of this book is that Americans do not have an ethnic identity, nor a religious identity. We have a philosophical identity. Our principles, based on Enlightenment philosophy, are who we are. If we abandon our principles we lose our identity as Americans.

Domestic Surveillance

Surveillance of our enemies is essential to our domestic security. We need to know what the enemy is planning, what their capabilities are, learn their tactics and strategy to more effectively combat them. But our government has extended surveillance from our enemies to our citizens. Security experts explain the nuances of domestic surveillance through scanning telephone conversations and emails looking for key words or phrases. But they listen to everything. Without warrants and only feeble internal oversight. Are we sacrificing essential liberty? The answer does not require a congressional hearing but only a single syllable: yes or no.

Edifice of Trust

"Enhanced" Interrogation

Americans do not torture or come close to torturing people. We do not parse words to redefine torture. Our principles assert the equality of all people not just citizens. Non-citizens and even our enemies deserve respectful treatment. They do not have rights as we know them because they are not citizens of the social contract. They do not reside within our edifice of trust. But they are still human beings and our principles require us to treat them civilly. Torturing people demeans us; it lessens us in our own eyes and in the eyes of the world. We can only gain the respect of the world by sticking to our principles.

Metastasized Terror

In early 2017 US Marines were sent to Syria to fight against ISIS (Islamic State or ISIL). This is in addition to US Special Forces that have been there in support of Iraqi and Kurdish troops. President Trump has vowed to wipe out ISIS and its terror network.

This is all well and good. ISIS and its followers are truly evil. But wiping out ISIS will not put an end to terror. ISIS itself is an outgrowth of the defeat of Al-Qaeda in Iraq by the US surge in 2007. Al-Qaeda in Iraq had formed as part of the insurgency against the US-backed Iraqi government after the defeat of Saddam Hussein.

The point is that defeating ISIS should not be considered a defeat of radical Islamic extremism. Like a cancer Al-Qaeda has metastasized into many linked or inspired groups around the world including Boko Haram, the Taliban and Al-Shabaab. Many of these terror cells are Sunni Muslim followers of Salafism (itself an outgrowth of Wahhabism, a strict form of Islam practiced in Saudi Arabia). The Saudis pay billions of dollars to fund schools (madrassas) all around the world that preach this form of Islam. This has lead to an increase in the percentage of Muslims that follow this version of Islam, which is coincident with the rise of extremist terror. Fifteen of the nineteen hijackers on 9/11 were Saudis. Wahhabists will say that Wahhabi Islam does not support terror against civilians but it is a short step from Wahhabism to more radical Salafism.

Edifice of Trust

<u>America or Ummah?</u>

Not all terrorists are jihadis, but most recent terror events around the world have been perpetrated by Islamic jihadis. There have been several terror attacks and attempted attacks in the United States by Muslim citizens or residents, including a knife attack and several bombs just six weeks before the election. In addition, a number of Muslims, including American citizens, have journeyed to the Middle East and Africa to join ISIS and Al-Shabaab. While Muslims have integrated better into the United States than in Europe, doubt remains. 47% of Muslims in America consider themselves Muslim first and Americans second according to a Pew Research Poll. The concept of the Islamic community (Ummah) as decreed by Muhammad in the Charter of Medina requires solidarity among Muslims over tribe or state. Christians and the followers of other religions do not face this potential conflict of interest because they can separate church and state. This is more difficult in Islam and, as a result, it undermines the trust necessary for the social contract. The lone wolf attacks by Muslims in the United States are intended to divide the Muslim American community from the rest of the citizens in the social contract. Muslim Americans need to be proactive in assuring fellow citizens that they are worthy of trust.

Edifice of Trust

Consequences

What are the consequences of living up to our principles? It will mean civilian casualties. There is no way around it. Torture does obtain actionable information. Actionable but tainted. Domestic surveillance has discovered spies and terrorists among us. Forgoing the use of torture and domestic surveillance will mean that we have less intelligence about the enemy and their plans. This will result in more civilian and military casualties. The politicians in Washington will not tell you this. They want you to believe that they can prevent this so that such events "will never happen again".

It will happen again. No amount of torture or domestic surveillance can assure that domestic terror attacks can be totally stopped. There is a heavy price to pay for this attempt to increase our security. It is our freedom: our essential liberty. The religious among us might say our very souls. If, in order to defeat our enemy, we must become more like them then we have lost and they have won[8].

---

8. The purpose of terror is to erode the trust among citizens that is the basis for the edifice of trust that holds the American Social Contract together. The innocent lives they take are only collateral damage in their goal to destroy western civilization. Our War on Terror is not doing much better than our War on Drugs and like our War on Drugs we need to do some major rethinking on how we execute our War on Terror.

Edifice of Trust

Chapter 11

What Works

What Works

Progressives are so focused on making the world look like the social paradise they envision that they will entertain almost any strategy in order to achieve their goal. Let's assume the goal is that the percentage of black students at elite colleges is equal to their percentage of the overall population. A worthy goal, indeed! Their response is to create a program such as affirmative action to require those elite colleges to accept more black students into their school. If, as they obviously assume, the sole reason that the percentage of black students is low is due to discrimination then these solutions would work very well. If, however, the reason that blacks are underrepresented at these institutions is more complex (as invariably is the case) then the chosen equal opportunity program may be less effective than planned, or it may be a total failure or (worse) it may have unintended consequences that are worse than the initial problem.

On March 23, 2016 at a town hall meeting with young people in Argentina President Obama stated:

Edifice of Trust

"I guess to make a broader point, so often in the past there's been a sharp division between left and right, between capitalist and communist or socialist. And especially in the Americas, that's been a big debate, right? Oh, you know, you're a capitalist Yankee dog, and oh, you know, you're some crazy communist that's going to take away everybody's property. And I mean, those are interesting intellectual arguments, but I think for your generation, you should be practical and just choose from what works. You don't have to worry about whether it neatly fits into socialist theory or capitalist theory -- you should just decide what works."

President Obama went on to praise Raul Castro for the accomplishments of his communist government. It is clear that President Obama makes no clear distinction between the American democratic free market system and socialism/communism. His philosophy is outcomes-based not process-based. Under this line of thinking if you don't like the outcome you arbitrarily change the outcome rather than fix the process. If the income distribution is not as equal as you like you simply take money from the wealthy and give it to the poor. Problem solved. If minority kids can't get into a good college because they went to crappy high schools then mandate that colleges accept a certain percentage of minority students for reasons of diversity. Problem solved.

Or is it? If poor people receive the money taken away from talented, educated, hard-working people then what will they do in order to further improve their economic situation? Hone their talents, get educated or work hard? I think not. They will try to elect politicians that will give them even more of other peoples' money. And making colleges accept poorly educated minority students doesn't solve the problem of the substandard education they got from the crappy schools they come from. There is growing evidence that these unprepared kids don't do well in college or get their degree. So the "solution" is mere window dressing that does nothing to solve the problem. Furthermore, these "solutions" come from government programs making the beneficiaries ever more dependent on government and in need of more "solutions".

Edifice of Trust

There is a moral and ethical problem that is a direct consequence of an excessive reliance on results. The reason that some outcomes differ from those desired can be due to multiple factors. The oft-cited gender pay gap is attributed to discrimination against women and legislation that has been proposed to remedy this situation reflects this assumption. It is true that there is discrimination against (and sometimes for) women, but that is only one of the many factors affecting the pay gap. Other factors include time off for child rearing, different work priorities and job specialization. Forcing a result (equal pay) as if only one factor caused the entire problem creates potential new injustices in those cases where other factors are at play.

There are also unintended consequences for this type of policy making. Affirmative action in hiring can result in ratios of minority employees similar to those in the general population but also taints all minority employees as not achieving their position on merit but from affirmative action. A truly talented, educated and motivated minority employee would be tainted with the same broad brush as other, less qualified, minority employees. Peer perceptions at work can have a big influence on many aspects of employee performance and satisfaction.

But poor policies and unintended consequences are not the worst results of outcomes-based policymaking. Great evil has been perpetrated because of a results-based focus. In order to achieve his goal of collectivization of the economy of the Soviet Union, Stalin ordered the elimination of the kulaks (small farmers) as a class. Aleksandr Solzhenitsyn estimated that as many as six million people died as a result (the Soviets admitted to only 700,000 deaths). Mao's attempt at collectivization (the Great Leap Forward) resulted in millions of deaths (some estimates as high as 45 million).

All these are examples of policies using the coercive power of the state to achieve a state defined outcome or approved goal. The state will strive to achieve such goal by any means necessary ("what works" as defined by president Obama) and will increase the amount of coercive force when outcomes vary from the expected results.

Edifice of Trust

A principled policy must strive to achieve a goal by actions that fall within the founding principles. If the goal is not achieved we must look to the cause of the variance from the intended result. This self-correcting mechanism does not exist under the "whatever works" philosophy. When a government program does not achieve the intended result, the progressive solution is more government programs, not a re-evaluation of the program to understand the underlying causes of the failure.

Finding real solutions is hard work and can involve telling people that they are part of the problem and need to change what they are doing in order to be part of the solution (like lowering the out-of-wedlock birthrate that is itself an unintended consequence of lenient welfare and tax policy "solutions"). This is not easy and it takes real leadership and honesty. But it is the only thing that really works.

President Trump also believes in what works solutions. He is very focused on outcomes and in "winning" as he defines it. Browbeating the Carrier air-conditioning company, and bribing them with tax incentives, saved about 700 jobs in Indiana. But the underlying causes that motivated Carrier to want to relocate their manufacturing in Mexico remain. If these underlying causes are allowed to persist, the Trump presidency will be littered with all sorts of ad hoc solutions. Each "solution" will be distinct and unique. It will be impossible to determine the principles behind these "solutions". Each solution will be touted by the White House as a win. But what legacy will they leave to succeeding administrations?

The Trump presidency is focused on instituting a wide-ranging series of reforms in order to "drain the swamp" that Washington DC has come to represent. I fear, however, that these reforms will be based on a preferred outcome and then jury-rigged in order to achieve that goal, rather than basing reforms on our founding principles and trusting in the result. The missteps of the early Trump White house have been have been in areas where the proposed outcomes have been blurred by unintended consequences and which were not clearly based on American principles.

Edifice of Trust

Fairness

President Obama's town hall meeting in Argentina was illustrative because it revealed the essential nature of the progressive movement. In his discussion, President Obama dismisses as irrelevant the philosophical and ideological bases for both capitalism and Marxism. The only criterion to be applied is "what works". But how do you determine what it is that you want to work? Progressives, lacking principles on which to base their preferred policies, rely on doing what is "fair". A $15 minimum wage is "fair". A woman's right to choose (i.e.; have an abortion) is "fair". Mandating employers to provide healthcare for workers is "fair".

There are two problems with this approach to policy making. The first is that the concept of fairness is not based on universally agreed-upon values or any objective standard. It is very subjective. What is fair to one person may not be fair to another. A $15 minimum wage (deemed by progressives to be a living wage) may seem fair to an uneducated, unmotivated worker but may not seem fair to a fast food franchise owner who is hard pressed to get $15 in value out of such workers for the hours they are being paid. An abortion may be "fair" for the woman but it is certainly not fair to the fetus. And why should employers be responsible for providing healthcare for employees? What started out as a benefit to attract good employees (like company cars and other "perqs") has become an onerous government mandated burden that many employers cannot afford.

Edifice of Trust

The fact is that fairness is a poor standard to use for policy making. At its roots, fairness is not based on the reasoned thinking of adults, but on the subjective opinions of children. Any parent taking their child to the playground will be pelted with repeated requests of adult intervention to make the other children play fairly, or to share fairly, or any other of the plethora of childish requests for "fair" treatment. Each child has his or her own idea of what "fair" means and appeals to the authority (Mom) to enforce their idea of what is "fair". This is the same form of intervention that progressives are asking the government to make.

The second great problem that arises from the use of fairness as a standard for policy making is how opposing sides of a proposed "fair" policy initiative characterize each other. If the proponents of a "fair" policy are good people motivated by good intentions (as progressive deem themselves to be), then opponents to the policy <u>must</u> be bad people motivated by bad intentions. You cannot have reasoned discussions of proposed policies if the presumption of one side is that the other side is acting in bad faith.

This becomes very apparent when you listen to progressives' complaints about any contentious policy discussion. The other side is greedy, they hate women, they want their employees to die. This ad-hominem type argument makes meaningful discussion impossible.

The beauty of Adam Smith's "invisible hand" guiding economic activity is that it does not depend on the motivations of the participants.

"It is not from the benevolence of the butcher, the brewer, or the baker that we expect our dinner, but from their regard to their own interest."
Adam Smith

An outcomes-based policy must rely on subjective fairness enforced by a superior power (whether Mom or the government). This is very different from the role of government envisioned by the Founders. To them, the role of government was to guarantee the equality of opportunity not of outcomes (outcomes would vary according to the individual). It is true that our government has not fulfilled this responsibility to the extent that it should. A poorly educated kid from a single parent household in a crime-infested neighborhood does not have an equal opportunity compared to a kid from the suburbs but a quota does not provide a solution. The real solution lies elsewhere and requires real hard work to achieve.

Progressives would have us throw out our principles and focus solely on outcomes. What works, as President Obama stated in Argentina, a country devastated by this type of thinking. It is intellectually lazy to discard principles and to create subjectively "fair" outcomes through government fiat and then say you have created a better society. It is much more difficult to get at the root causes that create unequal opportunity. This can only be done by constantly rededicating ourselves to our founding principles to create this better society.

The Virginia Declaration of Rights written in 1776 says it best:

That no free government, or the blessings of liberty, can be preserved to any people but by a firm adherence to justice, moderation, temperance, frugality, and virtue <u>and by frequent recurrence to fundamental principles</u> (emphasis mine).

Trump on Fairness

President Trump focuses on fairness even more than progressives. Press attacks on his policies or actions are "unfair" or "dishonest". Manufacturers that make rational, legal decisions to relocate their facilities overseas are "unfair". And like the progressives, he considers the people behind these actions as bad because they are unfair. He gets angry and lashes out at them on his Twitter account calling them fake, losers and the enemies of the people (conflating the interest of the people and his own personal interests, as is often the case with populists).

Basing policies and reforms on fairness instead of principles is likely going to produce a hodgepodge of confusing and conflicting regulations that

Edifice of Trust

create negative unintended consequences and no guidance as to how this fits into a philosophy of government.

Edifice of Trust

The Inconvenience of the Rule of Law

The "what works" philosophy doesn't just impact minorities and other progressive programs. In early 2016, the US Treasury announced new regulations governing corporate mergers known as inversions. Inversions are mergers of a US corporation with a foreign company where the merged company's domicile will be outside the United States, usually in a country with a low corporate tax rate. Inversions have been labeled "treasonous" and the companies doing them as "Benedict Arnolds" because they result in US firms paying lower taxes.

The US Treasury in the Obama administration issued new regulations designed to block the proposed merger of Pfizer (an American company) with Allergan (an Irish company). The regulations were very effective (they "worked" as defined by President Obama) and the companies dropped their plans to merge. The new regulations were not based on law or on precedent, but were concocted to paper over the problem of a dysfunctional US tax system. They were based on administrative actions and reinterpretations of regulations that then Treasury Secretary Lew had previously stated he couldn't legally do (I guess President Obama enlightened him on "what works").

It doesn't matter whether you believe tax inversions are a good thing or a bad thing. Here is the problem. Both the New York Times and the Wall Street Journal report that these new regulations could have been challenged in court with a good likelihood of prevailing. But that did not happen. It would be immensely costly and time-consuming to attempt to challenge these rules in

Edifice of Trust

court (a federal court where judges are appointed by the administration). Some of these court cases last decades and cost tens of millions of dollars (the Fallbrook case over water rights began in 1951 and is still being litigated). Unlike businesses, the government does not do a cost/benefit analysis of future litigation so it can continue to push a case forward almost indefinitely while the costs to the other side continuously increase. Any public company challenging these regulations would be betraying its fiduciary duty to its shareholders by spending so much money and management time on an effort with such an uncertain outcome.

What has happened here is that the Obama administration used the coercive power of the state to force these two companies to do what it desired without regard to the rule of law. What the companies were attempting to do was legal according to current law and precedent, quite apart from whether you think it was the "right" thing to do or not. But from the government's perspective the outcome was "fair" because it achieved the government's goals.

This is precisely the type of oppressive action the Founders feared when they drafted the Constitution. President Obama believed that the lack of action by the legislative branch gave him de facto power to act. As a constitutional scholar and senior lecturer at the University of Chicago Law School President Obama surely understands the Constitution very well. But he was using this knowledge to circumvent the Constitution in order to pursue his progressive agenda.

Similar to President Obama, President Trump is threatening to use executive actions to obtain desired outcomes that will meet the test of "fairness" according to the president. Already our allies and trading partners are quavering at the prospect of some outcome being declared "unfair' and subject to an unknown but possibly draconian change in traditional US policy. President Trump has rattled our NATO allies because of his declaration the allies' deficient defense spending will cause a rupture of this important alliance (even as Russian President Putin moves troops to the border of our Baltic allies).

This uncertainty will carry over into the business community affecting business investment, employment and economic growth. In the early phase of

Edifice of Trust

the Trump presidency the stock market has rallied at the prospect of lower taxes and less regulation. But if the White House is going to second-guess every business decision based on the president's definition of fairness, then investment will dry up, employment will stagnate and economic growth will falter. This is not the Rule of Law, it is the rule of man (one man).

Edifice of Trust

What Works for Presidential Campaigns

Both of our major presidential candidates in the 2016 election had their own litany of campaign promises of what (they think) works. These policies are not based on American principles but on what is deemed "fair" by the candidates or their supporters.

My first book, *Principled Policy*, dealt extensively with the concept of fairness. In it, I argued that fairness does not make a good standard for developing government policies. Fairness is inherently subjective. What one person believes is fair another person might perceive as unfair. Fairness lies deep with the instinctual brain. In the dog-eat-dog primeval world, the individual that doesn't get its fair share might perish. In times of scarcity many individuals in the group may perish, whether the group is a pack of wolves or a band of nomads. This kind of fairness is visceral; "unfair" actions threaten survival and generate anger.

Freedom and fairness are incompatible. In a freely negotiated settlement of differences each side usually has to give up some of their demands or points. Giving up on these positions is "unfair" but not "too unfair" since, if it were too unfair, there would be no agreement. Mr. Trump and his followers would call this "losing". Mrs. Clinton and her following would call this "unfair".

Only coercion can achieve this kind of fairness. Sometimes you have to make people do the "right thing", as if they were little children. In order to make people do the "right thing" we need the red guards, PC police, Venezuelan

Edifice of Trust

colectivos, etc. A recent example was the demand by the Obama administration that schools allow transgender people to use the bathroom corresponding to their gender identity or face the loss of federal funding. Whether or not you agree with the objective you must admit that the government is using coercion and state power to enforce what it has determined is "fair". The government may be promoting this action because it is kind and benevolent. Or it may be pushing a political agenda that will pay off in votes in future elections.

The Trump campaign promised to reduce the US trade deficit and would do whatever it takes to do so without regard for the underlying causes of the deficit. Companies move operations overseas in order to be able to compete in a very competitive global business environment. Requiring them to reshore their operations would be deemed fair by US blue collar workers but not very fair by the shareholders of US corporations. Employing import substitution strategies to resolve this dilemma, Mr. Trump would likely have to raise tariff barriers to protect the US industries from foreign competition. This would mollify the shareholders but would be perceived as "unfair" by millions of consumers who would have to pay higher prices for shoddy products (to say nothing about foreign producers who have been shut out of the US market).

Mrs. Clinton's progressive Democratic platform was a laundry list of "what works" to make things "fair". The platform had 42 references to "fair". "Fair" taxes, "fair" trade, "fair" wages, you name it. In order to achieve each of these fairnesses the government would have to use coercion to make people or institutions do the "right thing". $15 an hour has been deemed a "fair" minimum wage for burger-flippers because it can support a family with around $30,000 in wages, even if the flipper is a teenage kid living at home. But while employment is growing across the country, employment in cities that have enacted new minimum wage laws are seeing lower growth than other cities according to the Paychex Small Business Employment Survey. No doubt government could use coercion to try and block other anti-fairness actions of these employers such as raising prices, laying off workers, using technology to increase productivity or going out of business.

Edifice of Trust

This is the conundrum of the "what works" philosophy. Actions based on "fairness" instead of principle generate unintended consequences that need to be addressed, also in the interest of "fairness". These actions require other patches to fix the inevitable inequities that result from these actions. The result is a complex, opaque system that only benefits the insiders and elites that have access to the reins of power. I have seen this in corrupt Latin American countries. I also see this in America now. The complexity and opaqueness of the US economy does not arise from the principles of the free market economic system, but the actions of special interest groups in collusion with the government that are seeking "fairness" (privilege, actually) for the members of their group whether they be corporations or unions.

Populists and progressives wrap themselves in a banner of fairness with little regard for the principles behind the American flag. We must abandon this fruitless pursuit of what is "fair" and "what works" and return to our American principles. Through the American Social Contract we can agree on a system that is "not too unfair" and that works pretty well for everyone instead of using state coercion to pick winners and losers.

Edifice of Trust

The Trump Presidency

The 2016 election came down to a Hobson's choice between two candidates that each utilized a "what works" approach to solving America's great problems instead of a principled approach based on America's founding principles. The nasty, divisive campaigns gave short shrift to addressing America's real problems and devolved into an unmitigated series of personal attacks interspersed with privacy hacks and leaks that revealed underlying tawdry nature of the candidates and their campaigns.

The idea that Donald Trump could actually win the 2016 election and become the 45th president of the United States was inconceivable. He had a slapdash campaign team and only a rudimentary grass roots organization. But he was an indefatigable campaigner crisscrossing the country to lead sold-out rallies of cheering supporters. He had only a reductive understanding of the issues facing our country and offered simplistic solutions to these deeply complex problems. But these simplistic solutions appealed to his base of supporters.

More importantly he portrayed himself as the agent of change and painted Mrs. Clinton as the lackey of the status quo, talking about change but already sold out to the elites and the global establishment. The results were telling. As predicted, Mrs. Clinton handily won the progressive bastions on the east and west coast, but vast swaths of the interior went to the Trump camp. Mrs. Clinton won the popular vote by over three million votes but lost the all-important vote of the Electoral College.

Edifice of Trust

The math was irrefutable. Each Electoral College vote in California represents 696,954 people while in Wyoming each vote only represents 194,219 people. Mrs. Clinton's strategy of concentrating on populous states with large metropolitan centers was very inefficient compared to Mr. Trump's strategy of focusing on "flyover" country. Mrs. Clinton's supporters cried foul since she won the popular vote but the Electoral College functioned precisely as the Founders intended (at least on their second try). The Electoral College is designed to keep one or two states from dominating the entire country. If you exclude California and New York, Donald Trump won the popular vote.

Populism (left & right) vs. (l.c.) republicanism
The Founders feared unfettered democracy. John Adams famously said

"Remember, democracy never lasts long. It soon wastes, exhausts, and murders itself. There never was a democracy yet that did not commit suicide."

They feared that the majority (the common folk) would tyrannize the minority and would vote benefits for themselves that would exhaust the economic resources of the country. They feared that the majority could be easily swayed by persuasive orators such as Pericles in Athens and the string of populists that peppered the late Roman Republic. They had been trained in the classics and knew what history predicted would be the fate of the American experiment with democracy.

But the concept that the people have the right to govern themselves is too powerful to deny. Who else can claim such right except the through the Hobbesian use of force to exert the will of one person over another? So in addition to the right of the people to choose their leaders, the Founders created a republic that included checks and balances that would reduce the vulnerability of the country to temporary passions that can be used to manipulate the people.

Despite the Founders' fears, our republic has lasted 228 years. It has not only been transformed from an agricultural backwater to the most powerful country in the world, it has also remained a beacon of freedom for all the other peoples of the world not so blessed as we.

Before we congratulate ourselves overmuch however, we must reflect on our remaining vulnerability to temporary passions. Perhaps John Adams was not wrong but only made a mistake in the timing of our suicide. The 2016 election was populist battle on the right and on the left and we were doomed to the election of a "what works" populist leader no matter which major party we chose. Are these the first steps down the road to political suicide? or will the checks and balances put in place by the Founders so long ago come to our aid once again?

The Trump Presidency

Mr. Trump is a businessman who has very limited experience with public policy. He is accustomed to making donations to politicians in order to gain influence so he knows how things work. The question is: does he know how things are <u>supposed</u> to work? These are the principled questions we must ask any leader: what are your principles and how do you intend to implement them?

Mr. Trump's ghostwritten book, *The Art of Deal*, explains it all. To President Trump, everything is a negotiation. Position statements are just stratagems. While this may be a good technique in a business deal it is no way to lead a country. America is more than a deal and stands for more than just winning.

Where Mrs. Clinton looked out at America and saw victims, Candidate Trump looked out and saw losers. There isn't really much difference between victims and losers although each campaign had its own identifiable target market of victims/losers.

Mr. Trump also has a Hobbesian view of government. He appears impatient with the slow, unwieldy democratic process and wants to rule by fiat. He calls legislators all sorts of unprintable names. But government is not a business and the role of government is not to win or make a profit. To repeat what I said at the beginning of this book, the role of government is to maintain the American Social Contract so that citizens can have trust in their dealings and interactions with other citizens.

A Principled Reform Strategy

Initially when I wrote my first book, <u>Principled Policy</u>, I had thought that the 2016 election would be an inflection point where the United States would either return to its Founding Principles and achieve new heights of economic growth and national power or sink into an abyss of ever-creeping socialism. Increasingly I am thinking that the best we can hope for out of this recent election is a period of transition, a period of deconstruction of the status quo in preparation for a future reconstruction of a new paradigm of governance. At least that will give us time to further chart a return to America's founding principles.

President Trump has initiated his presidency with an all-out assault on the traditional democratic structures of Washington. From this book and my earlier book, it is clear that some demolition is necessary ("draining the swamp" as President Trump calls it). But will what emerges from the ashes be institutions that will last us for a century or two into the future or will the changes be ephemeral only to dissipate like so many tendrils of smoke? Perhaps President Trump will surprise us (again) and rise to the occasion as required by his high office. But we must also be prepared for a less benign outcome. Populism has a horrifying tendency to slide into authoritarianism. President Trump reminds me more of Berlusconi than Mussolini but we citizens must be ready to resist actions that run counter to our founding principles, including those enumerated in the Bill of Rights.

To be lasting, reform must be based on principles. As a people we must make our elected representatives aware of the need for principled-based reform. Spread the Word!

Essential Reading

Essential Reading from Principled Policy

The Road to Serfdom, Freidrich Hayek

The Wealth of Nations, Adam Smith

Common Sense, Thomas Paine

Second Treatise of Government, John Locke

The Constitution of the United States

The Declaration of Independence

Democracy in America, Alexis de Tocqueville

This Time is Different, Carmen M. Reinhart and Kenneth Rogoff

The Black Swan, Nassim Taleb

Capitalism, Socialism and Democracy, Joseph Schumpeter

The Commanding Heights, Daniel Yergin and Joseph Stanislaw

Thinking Fast and Slow, Daniel Kahneman

The Great Degeneration, Niall Ferguson

Coming Apart: The State of White America 1960-2010, Charles Murray

Edifice of Trust

A Troublesome Inheritance, Nicholas Wade

Misbehaving, The Making of Behavioral Economics, Richard H. Thaler

A Capitalism for the People, Luigi Zingales

Why Nations Fail, Daron Acemoglu and James Robinson

Essential Reading for Edifice of Trust

The Difference, Scott E. Page

The Clash of Civilizations and the Remaking of World Order, Samuel P. Huntington

A Crude Look at the Whole, John H. Miller

The Unheavenly City Revisited, Edward C. Banfield

The Peloponnesian War, Thucydides

About the Author/Acknowledgements

Victor C. Bolles

Victor is the author of the groundbreaking book, *Principled Policy* that analyses the American Social Contract and builds a framework of how to understand the most important public policy issues of our time. He has followed up that important work with his new book, Edifice of Trust, looking at how the important social issues of our time relate to the American Founding Principles. He also looks at the positions of the presidential candidates in the 2016 election and offers insights on how to view their principal (as opposed to principled) policy positions.

Victor has worked in the Office of Technical Assistance of the US Treasury Department for over twelve years specializing in advising foreign governments on the issuance and management of government debt. He worked throughout Central America and the Caribbean and was resident for eight years in Honduras and El Salvador.

Prior to joining Treasury, Victor was an independent investment banker working out of San Antonio, TX. Victor worked at Citibank for many years in New York, Mexico City, Quito, Ecuador and Lagos, Nigeria where he was head of the investment bank and regional treasurer. His first job after graduate school was with Swiss Bank Corporation (now a part of UBS).

Victor has lived overseas for 16 years, speaks Spanish fluently and has traveled extensively. Victor has an MBA in Finance from the University of Michigan. He is married to Diane and has three children and three grandchildren

(This book and its contents are the sole work of Victor Bolles in his capacity as a private citizen and should not be considered to be a statement of policies or opinions of the Department of the Treasury.)

Read Victor's blog at:
www.edificeoftrust.com/principled-policy-blog

www.edificeoftrust.com

Acknowledgements

I want to thank Geoffrey Finch for his patient and diligent review of my early drafts of this book. His rigorous review made me rethink many of my arguments and forced me to strengthen many of my analyses.

www.ingramcontent.com/pod-product-compliance
Lightning Source LLC
Chambersburg PA
CBHW031051180526
45163CB00002BA/785